Evangelism

For the Care of Souls

LEXHAM MINISTRY GUIDES

Evangelism

For the Care of Souls

SEAN MCGEVER

General Editor
Harold L. Senkbeil

LEXHAM PRESS

Evangelism: For the Care of Souls

Lexham Ministry Guides

Lexham Press, 1313 Commercial St., Bellingham, WA 98225

LexhamPress.com

Print ISBN 9781683596899

Digital ISBN 9781683596905

Library of Congress Control Number 2022944139

Series Editor: Harold L. Senkbeil

Lexham Editorial: Todd Hains, Allisyn Ma, Cindy Huelat

Cover Design: Joshua Hunt, Brittany Schrock

Typesetting: Mandi Newell

Dedicated to Micah, Mike, and Dick,
messengers of the good news to me

Contents

ACTS 20:28

Pay careful attention to yourselves and
to all the flock, in which the Holy Spirit
has made you overseers, to care
for the church of God,
which he obtained
with his own
blood.

Series Preface

WHAT'S OLD IS NEW AGAIN.

The church in ages past has focused her mission through every changing era on one unchanging, Spirit-given task: the care of souls in Jesus' name. Christian clergy in every generation have devoted themselves to bringing Christ's gifts of forgiveness, life, and salvation to people by first bringing them to faith and then keeping them in the faith all life long.

These people—these blood-bought souls—are cared for just as a doctor cares for bodies. The first step is carefully observing the symptoms of distress, then diagnosing the ailment behind these symptoms. Only after careful observation and informed diagnosis can a physician of souls proceed—treating not the symptoms, but the underlying disease.

Attention and intention are essential for quality pastoral care. Pastors first attentively listen with Christ's ears and then intentionally speak with Christ's mouth. Soul care is a ministry of the Word; it is rooted in the conviction that God's word is efficacious—it does what it says (Isa 55:10–11).

This careful, care-filled pastoral work is more art than science. It's the practical wisdom of theology, rooted in focused study of God's word and informed by the example of generations past. It's an aptitude more than a skillset, developed through years of ministry experience and ongoing conversation with colleagues.

The challenges of our turbulent era are driving conscientious evangelists and pastors to return to the soul care tradition to find effective tools for contemporary ministry. (I describe this in depth in my book *The Care of Souls: Cultivating a Pastor's Heart.*) It's this collegial conversation that each author in this series engages—speaking from their own knowledge and experience. We want to learn from each other's insights to enrich the soul care tradition. How can we best address contemporary challenges with the timeless treasures of the Word of God?

IN THE LEXHAM MINISTRY GUIDES YOU WILL
meet new colleagues to enlarge and enrich your
unique ministry to better serve the Savior's sheep
and lambs with confidence. These men and women
are in touch with people in different subcultures
and settings, where they are daily engaged in learning the practical wisdom of the care of souls in real-
life ministry settings just like yours. They will share
their own personal insights and approaches to one
of the myriad aspects of contemporary ministry.

Though their methods vary, they flow from one
common conviction: all pastoral work is rooted
in a pastoral habitus, or disposition. What every
pastor does day after day is an expression of who
the pastor is as a servant of Christ and a steward
of God's mysteries (1 Cor 4:1).

Although the authors may come from theological traditions different than yours, you will find a
wealth of strategies and tactics for practical ministry you can apply, informed by your own confession of the faith once delivered to the saints
(Jude 1:3).

OUR LORD DOESN'T CALL US TO SUCCESS, as if
the results were up to us: "Neither he who plants
nor he who waters is anything, but only God who

gives the growth" (1 Cor 3:7). No, our Lord asks us to be faithful laborers in the service of souls he has purchased with his own blood (Acts 20:28).

Nor does our Lord expect us to have all the answers: "I will give you a mouth and wisdom" (Luke 21:15). Jesus, the eternal Word of the Father, is the Answer who gives us words when we need them to give to our neighbors when they need them. After all, Jesus sees deeper into our hearts than we do; he knows what we need. He is the Wisdom of God in every generation (1 Cor 1:24).

But wisdom takes time. The Lord our God creates, redeems, and sanctifies merely by his words. He could give us success and answers now, but he usually doesn't. We learn over time through challenges and frustrations—even Jesus grew over time (Luke 2:52). The Lexham Ministry Guides offer practical wisdom for the church.

MY PRAYER IS THAT YOU GROW IN HUMBLE appreciation of the rare honor and responsibility that Christ Jesus bestowed on you in the power and presence of his Spirit: "As the Father has sent me, even so I am sending you" (John 20:21).

Father in heaven, as in every generation you send forth laborers to do your work and equip them by your word, so we pray that in this our time you will continue to send forth your Spirit by that word. Equip your servants with everything good that they may do your will, working in them that which is well pleasing in your sight. Through Jesus Christ our Lord. Amen.

Harold L. Senkbeil, General Editor
September 14, 2020
Holy Cross Day

Prayer for Announcing the Word

Since the earliest days of the church, Christians have used Holy Scripture to shape and inform their prayer lives. The structured prayer below invites pastors and laity to pray for the announcement and reannouncment of the good news of the gospel to all people. It can be used by either individuals or groups—in which case a designated leader begins and others speak the words in bold font.

In the name of the Father, Son, and Holy Spirit.
Amen.

O Lord, open my lips,
And my mouth will declare your praise. *Ps 51:15*

Sing a new song to the Lord!
Let the whole earth sing to the Lord!

Sing to the LORD; praise his name.
**Each day proclaim the good news that
he saves.**

Publish his glorious deeds among the nations.
**Tell everyone about the amazing things
he does.**

O nations of the world, recognize the LORD;
**recognize that the LORD is glorious
and strong.**

Tell all the nations, "The LORD reigns!"
**The world stands firm and cannot be shaken.
He will judge all peoples fairly.** *Ps 96:1–3; 7, 10 NLT*

Let us pray.

That we may always proclaim of first importance
that Christ died for our sins according to
the Scriptures, and that he was raised on the
third day according to the Scriptures.
That we may rejoice that your Holy Spirit, who
raised Jesus from the dead, lives in us, and
beckons us to proclaim your power and
goodness to our families, neighbors, and all
people.

Lord, in your mercy,
Hear our prayer.

That whenever we speak, words may be given
us so that we will fearlessly make known the
mystery of the gospel.

That we will always be prepared to give an
answer to everyone who asks us to give the
reason for the hope that is in us with a spirit
of gentleness and respect.

That we will reject any merit of our works and
embrace that we did not receive the Spirit by
works of the law but by believing the good
news of your Son.

Lord, in your mercy,
Hear our prayer.

Our Father who art in heaven
Hallowed be thy name,
Thy kingdom come,
Thy will be done on earth as it is in heaven;
Give us this day our daily bread;
And forgive us our trespasses as we forgive
    those who trespass against us;
And lead us not into temptation,
But deliver us from evil.
For thine is the kingdom and the power, and
    the glory forever and ever.
Amen. *Matt 6:9–13*

Almighty God our Savior, you desire that none should perish, and you have taught us through your Son that there is great joy in heaven over every sinner who repents. Grant that our hearts may ache for a lost and broken world. May your Holy Spirit work through our words, deeds, and prayers, that the lost may be found and the dead be made alive, so that all your redeemed may rejoice eternally around your throne, through Jesus Christ, your Son, our Lord, who lives and reigns with You and the Holy Spirit, one God, now and forever.

Amen.

The Lord bless us, protect us from all evil, and bring us to everlasting life.

Amen.

CHAPTER 1

Announcing Jesus

*The prophet Isaiah was speaking about John when
he said, "He is a voice shouting in the wilderness,
'Prepare the way for the L*ORD*'s coming!
Clear the road for him!'"*
—*Matthew 3:3 NLT*

"THE GREATEST TRICK THE DEVIL ever pulled
was convincing the world he didn't exist," says
Keyser Söze in the movie *The Usual Suspects*. I
argue one of the greatest tricks the devil ever pulled
was convincing Christians they only need to hear
the gospel once. The pastoral practice of evangelism has eroded into a skeleton of itself and seemingly only has relevance for our skeleton days too.
Evidence of hit-and-run evangelism is rampant.
Many people have tucked into their back pockets

what they think is their "get out of hell" free card to retrieve later. Other converts were sold an evangelistic bill of goods that makes promises for God that God never made. Ministers often have the difficult task of going backward with converts to retrace their initial steps in order to move forward into the life of faith. When ministers do this repair work, the evangelistic task is not finished—instead, it repeats. The devil never takes a day off. Like the roads in my city, repair is needed constantly. The church requires a revival of lifelong evangelism to nourish the souls God brings into our midst. The Lord gives us the great privilege of announcing and reannouncing Jesus Christ, the word of God, as the good news.

Pastors have at their disposal a myriad of words to care for souls. The announcement that the crucified Jesus has been raised from the dead—Jesus is Lord of all—is the balm, ointment, and cure for our hearts throughout life. This announcement is central to the beginning of the Christian life: Christ carried our sins to the cross and conquered them through his resurrection. Our baptisms remind us of this. This announcement is central to the life of faith; whatever our path, joy, or trial, Jesus is Lord.

Our regular partaking of the Lord's Supper reminds us of this. This announcement is central to the end of our life: our resurrection day awaits, as it did our Lord; our funerals celebrate this fact. Evangelism is not a special task outsourced to a unique group of people, though it can be. Evangelism is not a one-time confrontational conversation, though it can be. Evangelism is at the heart of the ongoing work of pastoral care, inviting outsiders into the flock of the church and reminding insiders of the heart of the ongoing life of faith.

Front Row Seats

Front row seats are the best. You hear and notice things that you would never experience from farther back. When I'm in the front row of a basketball game, I hear the chatter of the players and referees, the gasping for breath between plays, the sweat falling on the hardwood—those in the front row get to absorb the humanity of the moment. When I'm in the front row of a theatrical performance, I feel the power and delicacy of a voice nurtured through years of guidance and practice. I notice the tape marking the stage to help performers shine in the spotlights. I see the intricate

3

patterns woven into garments that are hardly noticeable from the section behind me.

One of my favorite front row seats is one that you can't purchase. In fact, it's priceless. I get goosebumps just thinking about the anticipation I get when I walk up to take my place at this occasion. The music begins, everyone rises from their seats, and then it starts: the bride walks down the aisle. I hardly believe that I get to see the bride in the same moment her groom sees her. I see the two of them in their first glimpse of each other on their wedding day. In that moment, I often look over my shoulder at the groom as he is in awe of his long-awaited bride. Then, I look back at the bride with her eyes locked on her groom. One of the rookie mistakes I made in officiating marriages was to forget to tell the audience to sit down afterward. All my focus was on what was happening right in front of me; I couldn't think about anything else. I was overtaken, as if only the three of us were standing there. In a flash, I pronounced them husband and wife. Shortly before, they arrived single, but now they depart united.

My role in a wedding ceremony isn't merely a front row seat; it is by far the best seat in the house.

When I officiate a wedding, I play a short-term role in a life-changing event. I repeat some words I chose for the occasion; I recite a few Scripture passages relevant for the event, but most of all, I watch and try to get out of the way of the story that God has written in their lives. The last thing I want to do is have their memories of that moment be about *me*.

This book is not about weddings; it is about evangelism. But, for a moment, I'd like you to think about evangelism through the lens of officiating a wedding. Evangelism can feel like you control the eternal destiny of another person's life. Not true. In a wedding, the officiant enters a story that is advanced, complicated, and well underway. The characters have gone through many twists and turns, and the wedding is merely a short chapter in a much longer story. Now, don't get me wrong, the wedding is important and essential to the story— without it the rest of the story would have a much different path. Yet, I often tell my engaged friends to put more energy into planning their marriage than their wedding.

Officiating a wedding is exciting; it is a front-row experience as an attendant. Evangelism is exciting; it

is also a front-row experience as an attendant—but just as an attendant. God saves; we do not.

I have been a vocational evangelist for the last three decades. I never intended to devote my professional life to this task, though I've been grateful and blessed to minister in this way. I grew up with little knowledge of Jesus and rarely stepped into a church in my childhood. When I was a junior in high school, a youth worker showed up at my school on a Monday at lunch with free pizza. That was one of the most important days of my life. A year later, I had been baptized, discipled, and was serving weekly in my church and reaching out to students at my old junior high school. The youth worker, Mike, was on his weekly route to deliver much more than pizza. He hoped and prayed to deliver a message that kids needed to hear: the message of the good news of Jesus Christ. The message landed right where it needed to: me.

After graduating college and working for a great technology company for a few years, my wife and I decided to quit our jobs and devote ourselves to recruiting, training, and equipping people to evangelize teenagers. I've learned that the ministry of evangelism is complex. The message of

Jesus Christ is so simple that a child can understand it and repeat it, yet it is so multilayered and powerful that I rarely feel that I can communicate it fully. The experience of the messenger (the evangelist) is a simple task: to tell God's story. Yet, my announcement of the good news interweaves with my own hesitation, doubt, and pride. Evangelism is an emotional roller coaster, at least for me.

Evangelism is never a self-initiated task. Evangelism, as we will see, requires a sender and a messenger. God is the sender, and the real messenger is not who you think it is. The real messenger is God. God sends the Holy Spirit, and people enabled by the Holy Spirit, as messengers appointed by God for this task. God told Moses to deliver a message to the Israelites when they were in bondage, at the foot of Sinai, and many other times. The message and the messenger were from God and delivered to the people of God through God's Spirit. Similarly, God used other prophets to deliver God's message. The Father chose his Son, Jesus of Nazareth, to deliver God's message: "The Spirit of the Lord is on me, because he has anointed me to proclaim good news to the poor.

He has sent me to proclaim freedom for the prisoners and recovery of sight for the blind, to set the oppressed free, to proclaim the year of the Lord's favor" (Luke 4:18–19).

At the outset of this book, I need to make a confession. I am embarrassed and ashamed that, for me, evangelism can be a self-serving activity. It can also be a self-defeating activity. Let me explain this a bit.

TEMPTATION

For whatever reason, I'm competitive. In sports, I strive to win and improve. In school and academics, I always strove to get 100 percent. I have thought a lot about my competitive and determined nature and have concluded that it is morally neutral—it is just a feature of how I think and work. The part that gets me in trouble is when my competitive nature interacts with my heart, my self-worth, my interactions with others, and with the Lord. This is why evangelism can be a dangerous task for me.

When I think about my impulse to evangelize others, my motivation exists somewhere in the overlap of my thankfulness to the Lord for saving me, my obedience to God's word to preach the gospel, and my competitive desire to "win" souls.

It is the last part that is most dangerous for me because it *could* be morally neutral, or even noble in some way, but my impulse to evangelize requires a confession that I do it sometimes for selfish purposes: I want to win.

I work frequently at outreach camps as a speaker and camp director where a report is due each time students depart from their time at camp. One of the questions on the form is: "How many students this week made a decision to follow Christ for the first time?" This simple question is a can of worms for me in so many ways. In the end, I usually ask someone else to give me a number; I write it in blindly and send the report. The question is a conundrum for me because my honest answer is: "Only God knows." The question also creates a mountain of biblical, theological, historical, and psychological issues for me that make my mind explode. The hardest part for me is a personal one; the question feels like a reflection of my self-worth, my performance, and my faith. On one hand, the question feels like a zero-sum game; if a certain number of students leave the camp following Christ, how many left the camp not following Christ? On the other hand, I can't help but believe a logical and theological evangelism fallacy:

correlation is causation. A person might or might not come to faith at the camp for a lot of reasons, all of which are outside of my control. Yet, that's not how it feels to me. And part of me blames Acts 14 for feeling this way.

In Acts 14, we read: "At Iconium Paul and Barnabas went as usual into the Jewish synagogue. There they spoke so effectively that a great number of Jews and Greeks believed" (Acts 14:1). This verse strikes me as odd for at least two reasons. First, Paul didn't aim to speak the gospel with "wisdom or eloquence" (1 Cor 1:17); people commented that he was "unimpressive and his speaking amounts to nothing" (2 Cor 10:10), and he admitted that he was "untrained as a speaker" (2 Cor 11:6). Second, is it possible to speak "so effectively" that people believe in Jesus? The previous chapter in Acts adds an additional layer of complexity for evangelists. Luke describes Paul's and Barnabas's speaking in Pisidian Antioch as such: "When the Gentiles heard this, they were glad and honored the word of the Lord; and all who were appointed for eternal life believed" (Acts 13:48).

So, which is it? Do people believe because they were "appointed for eternal life," or because people like Paul and Barnabas "speak so effectively"? I

believe the correct answer is yes. For example, Calvinists might explain that the speaking was effective because of effectual, efficacious, irresistible grace, but does this mean that the speaking was actually effective? Arminians might explain that the people were appointed to believe that day because God empowered Paul and Barnabas to speak "so effectively." Lutherans might emphasize the efficacious word of God, which was certainly a part of Paul's and Barnabas's message in Iconium and was highlighted explicitly in their ministry in Pisidian Antioch where "the word of the Lord spread throughout the whole region" (Acts 13:49). I could add additional perspectives, but we don't need to here. The goal of this book is not to sort that out; our task is different. Our goal is to think about how to care for souls as evangelists.

Evangelism and Evangelicalism

I want to explain what I mean when I use the word "evangelism." Evangelism is sharing the good news of God. The closest metaphor for evangelism is a messenger.

There are three ancient terms for sharing the Christian message: *marturein* ("bear witness"), *kērussein* ("proclaim"), and *euangelizesthai*

("evangelize")—though each of these concepts overlap in meaning. When Christians bear witness they witness to what they have seen and heard to those who ask them; this is akin to when a witness sits on the witness stand in court and is questioned regarding what they have experienced, seen, and heard. Bearing witness was frequently a response to friendly or adversarial curiosity or questioning. To proclaim the Christian message is to initiate the preaching or heralding of important news.

The verb "evangelize" means to bring or announce good news. The English words "gospel" and "evangelism" are related. When we take a closer look at the Greek noun for evangelism, *euangelion*, broken down as *eu-angelion*, we see that the Greek prefix *eu-* means "good" or "beautiful," while the second part, *angelion*, is a "message" or "messenger"—as in "angel," since an angel is a messenger from God. I like to say that evangelists are people who are messengers who bring the news that God is good. I don't say it aloud because it might seem a bit too much, but I picture evangelists as playing an angelic role as they deliver a gift directly from God in heaven to people on earth deeply in need of good news.

Mark starts with the good news itself: "The beginning of the good news [*euangelion*] about Jesus the Messiah, the Son of God" (Mark 1:1). Luke writes, "The angel [*angelos*] said to him [Zechariah], 'I am Gabriel. I stand in the presence of God, and I have been sent to speak to you and to tell you this good news [*euangelion*]" (Luke 1:19). Luke's wording shows the natural connection between an angel as a messenger and the substance of the message being good news.

Before we continue our discussion of evangelism, we need to weed out a few thorny issues with the concept of evangelism. First, we must distinguish evangelism from evangelicalism. Evangelicalism has its own thorny branches in recent years, perhaps most infamously, how conservative American politics have co-opted the legacy of evangelicalism. Modern American evangelicalism is just one facet of a movement with a long and influential history that dates back to the early eighteenth century.[1] Today, there are millions of evangelicals whose identity has little or nothing to do with conservative American politics.

Another thorny issue in evangelism is the accusation of manipulation. Evangelists are known for

high-pressure tactics to push hearers into responding to the gospel message. In 1960, Karl Barth accused well-known evangelical Billy Graham, whom he otherwise liked, as presenting "the gospel at gunpoint."[2] Charles Finney had much to do with the origin and trajectory of high-pressure tactics among evangelicals. In 1835, Finney championed three new measures of innovation in his revivals, the most well-known being the anxious seat.[3] The anxious seat was an actual seat or pew near the front of the revival meeting. Finney recommended saying, "There's the anxious seat. Come forward and vow that you are determined to be on the Lord's side." Finney also said, "If he is unwilling to do a small thing like that, then he is unwilling to do anything." Finney taught the anxious seat is "a public manifestation of determination to be a Christian," and that "in the newborn church baptism met this need."[4] Finney, the former lawyer, had no reservations about applying high-pressure tactics for the sake of evangelism.

A final introductory issue to explore related to the concept of evangelism is the word "evangelism" itself. The word "evangelist" has been in use for many centuries, as will be explored in chapter 4, but the word "evangelism" is a rather recent

term. It begins appearing in the English language in the early eighteenth century. For example, a 1708 dictionary defines evangelism as "a bringing of glad tidings."[5] While some might expect the word "evangelism" to be a common one in the eighteenth-century evangelical revivals, it isn't. John Wesley and George Whitefield do not use the word "evangelism."[6] The usage of the word "evangelism" grew slightly in the nineteenth century, but mostly in relation to the various discussions of the lasting effects of the evangelical revival. The word "evangelism" came into common parlance in the late nineteenth century.[7] Because people prior to the nineteenth century didn't use the word "evangelism," we need to look at "preaching," "catechesis," "missions," and "baptism."[8]

SLICES WITH CARL

Eight weeks ago, I trembled as I sent a text message to my friend Carl. I asked him if he had ever considered following Jesus Christ as his Lord and Savior. I trembled because I felt that my relationship with Carl would change as soon as I sent the message. When we care for souls, souls don't always like the attention they receive. Carl responded two days later, and our relationship *did* change.

For the previous six months, I met with Carl and a few others weekly at our local pizza spot Slices. The elderly Italian owner with flour dusting his well-worn apron asked us which slices we wanted, warmed them up in his oven, served them to us on plates, and then our group walked outside and grabbed a table. Each week, after catching up and eating, my friends knew I would ask an icebreaker question and discuss a passage from the Bible. Over the months we met, we talked about the existence, or nonexistence, of God, how humans differ from other animals in the world, the consequences of our choices, whether the world is better off with speed limits and stop signs, why Jesus is ranked by secular scholars as the most important human being to ever live, and how God's plan to change the world is to do it through people. In a nutshell, we worked through the metanarrative of Scripture: creation, fall, redemption, and restoration.

After months of meeting and discussion, I sensed that I should ask Carl if he considered himself a Christian. Carl is kind and hardworking, listens, asks good questions, and is thoughtful. Carl eagerly and thoughtfully engaged in our weekly discussions. If a churchgoer met Carl, they would

likely assume that Carl is a Christian. But I was fairly certain that Carl did not consider himself a Christian. He didn't grow up in a Christian family, and he had rarely had been in a church and didn't have much desire to return. Carl, by my estimation, believed that God existed, that Jesus must be God due to his resurrection, and that God has a significant purpose in the world for Christians. I had spent months building a relationship with Carl and having meaningful conversations with him. Carl knows that I value our friendship independently from our conversations about Jesus Christ, but I knew that if I asked him where he stood with Christ, Carl would feel like he was letting me down. It did not surprise me that Carl took two days to respond to my question. He responded thoughtfully and respectfully but also with a tinge of formality that changed the nature of our friendship. Carl told me that he did not want to follow Christ as his Savior, but that he appreciated our conversations. After that, Carl didn't come to our lunches for a month.

The story about Carl is also a story about me. I told you what I did, what it felt like, and some of the strategies and approaches I used in evangelism. But there is another story that I can't tell you about

because I really don't know the details well enough to share it with you. It is the story of Carl and God. My story with Carl comes from dozens of hours spent together. God's story with Carl comes from an eternal perspective. In my finite friendship with Carl, my function as an evangelist is to be a temporary messenger, a temporary witness, for an infinite God who has a persistent message and ongoing witness in Carl's life. I'm a messenger. God's the savior. Evangelism fails when we confuse the two.

Delivering the King's Message

Being a messenger of the good news can be a roller coaster of a task. Imagine for a moment the point of view of the servants in Jesus's parable of the wedding banquet in Matthew 22:1–14. In this parable, Jesus explains that the kingdom of heaven is like a king who prepared a wedding banquet for his son. But it isn't that simple. This is where the servants enter the story. The king tells the servants to deliver invitations to the wedding. The servants do their job, and in the first round of invitations, the guests refused to come.

Undeterred, the king commands the servants to deliver a second round of invitations, but this

time with a little bit of sizzle, adding that the food will be fantastic: oxen and fattened cattle are on the menu. As a messenger, the job is always easier if you have an exciting message to deliver, and what could be better than inviting people to a party with filet mignon? The servants must have been confused and frustrated when some of the guests "paid no attention and went off" (Matt 22:5).

I remember bringing my sixteen-year-old son's friends to one of the best Italian restaurants in the state, famous for their pizza, and one friend ordered mac and cheese and root beer—but at least he showed up. It can be incredibly frustrating when people don't pay attention and ignore important information. Most of the students in the classes I teach know that when we are reviewing before a test I give major hints about what will be on the exam. I say something like, "This part is something you should *really, really* pay attention to. *You might see it again soon.*" I'm not subtle. Later, when I'm grading the exams, it becomes clear which students didn't pay attention to my lectures or my review session. It is incredibly frustrating! I mark their responses accordingly and move on.

The second round of wedding banquet invitations includes a much more shocking response

than simply ignoring the invitation. Imagine being a messenger for a free party with steak for a prominent person and the invitee kills you! Being a messenger, which is to be an evangelist, is serious business. Indeed, martyrdom is not merely a memory from the early church, it continues today. The saying "don't shoot the messenger" exists for a reason. We know that Jesus is telling a parable, and the servants represent the Old Testament prophets who were harassed, rejected, and killed—likely Jesus has in mind his recently beheaded cousin and messenger John the Baptist (Matt 14:10).

I haven't experienced a violent response from someone when I have shared the gospel with them. The most common negative response I receive is that a friendship changes for the worse. I have counseled countless teenagers, college students, and early career people as they prepared anxiously to have "the talk" with their significant other about moving from being just friends to something more. The anxiety comes from the person knowing that the relationship will likely never be the same after the conversation. As difficult as it might feel, nearly every person I talk to about the possibility of this conversation ends up going through with it because they can't imagine never knowing how the

other person might respond. The risk of changing the nature of the friendship is worth knowing the response. If the stakes were higher, like they are for my fellow Christians in other parts of the world, I'm not sure how I would handle it, and I'm not sure if I want to find out. Evangelism comes with consequences.

How did the remaining servants feel when the king killed the murderers and burned their city (Matt 22:7)? I imagine they would have preferred to have their servant-friends alive. The king explains that those he invited did not deserve to come (22:8). Were the invitees deserving in the first place since the king was the one that invited them? A smart aleck messenger might stop the king to question his seemingly contradictory logic—the invitees are deserving *because* you invited them— but these questions are not the job of a messenger for the king. The job of a messenger for the king is to deliver the king's message. As the parable explains, the king already had another task for his messengers.

The king instructed the servants to invite "anyone," the "bad as well as the good" (Matt 22:10). The servants tore up the long list of names on their previous lists and gave their invitation message

to everyone they could find. We know that this parable, and the parables in the previous chapter (Matt 21), highlight Israel's persistent rejection of God's messengers and that the Lord's message is formally expanding to all people. There is another layer to the expansion of the king's invitation. The servants previously invited people who would naturally be invited to a lavish wedding for a king's son (22:2)—these are people who have fields and businesses (22:5), those who can pass on a free meal because they have their own food, and some who had enough power and confidence to kill royal messengers (22:6). The invitation now extends to the lowly, the people on the street corners, those whose names were not on an elite list.

From the perspective of the servants, the story should be finished by verse 10: "The wedding hall was filled with guests." The servants did their job; they delivered the king's message, and the king filled his banquet hall. Job done, right? Yes, their job *as messengers* was over. In fact, their job as messengers was finished not when the banquet was full but much earlier when they simply delivered the message—the messengers had no control over the invitees' responses. But I want to put you in the shoes of one specific messenger.

What would it be like to be the messenger who invited the man that arrived without wedding clothes who was tied up and thrown "outside, into the darkness, where there will be weeping and gnashing of teeth" (Matt 22:13)? Christians have struggled to make sense of why the man didn't have the proper clothes and why the king was so harsh toward him. The interpretive key likely is found in the concluding verse: "Many are invited, but few are chosen." Jesus's parabolic conclusion is an amalgam of human freedom and divine sovereignty, of which we do not know the recipe. I find Susan Grove Eastman's comments helpful: "On the one hand, human beings are responsible for responding positively to God's invitation and summons. On the other hand, final judgment is in the hands of God. The only character who speaks throughout the parable is the king, who thereby stands as the chief actor in the story."[9] The chief actor in the story is the king, true. Yet, as any servant knows, the servants have their own experience too.

The invitees initially ignored, mistreated, and even killed the servant-messengers, the evangelists of the king. Later invitees accepted the invitation given by the messengers, which must have

brought the messengers great relief and joy. But what about the messenger who invited the man who came underdressed and who was thrown out? I wonder if the messenger felt responsible for this disastrous result. Perhaps the messenger could have been clearer about the dress code. It seemed that everyone else had the proper clothes. If the messenger is anything like me, he would have analyzed a million what-ifs about his delivery of the king's message. I know I would have responded this way because I have delivered the good news of the king to thousands of people, many of whom seem to have accepted the invitation but, by all appearances, left the party. I beat myself up wondering what I did wrong, if my invitation was unclear, if I should have walked with them further into the king's house, if I should have held their hand firmer. In sum, I wanted to be more than a messenger—I wanted to control my friends' lives for them, I wanted to be God. This is one of the many downfalls of evangelism: when we try to be the king rather than the messenger.

So, what do we do as messenger-evangelists when we are eager to obey the king's orders to deliver the invitation and we are ignored or mistreated (and, Lord-willing, not killed)? Or, when

the invitation is accepted and some are kicked out of the party? What do we do when we find ourselves tempted to assume the role of the king when we are the messenger? The answer is found in retracing the footsteps and experiences of the one who "went into Galilee, proclaiming the good news of God. 'The time has come,' he said. 'The kingdom of God has come near. Repent and believe the good news!' " (Mark 1:14–15). Jesus is both the messenger and the king who was ignored, mistreated, killed, and for some of those who did accept his invitation, they were thrown out, even one of his most intimate friends: Judas. We remember that shortly before his ascension, his closest followers worshiped him, "but some doubted" (Matt 28:17).

Our motivation for evangelism must be a motivation to follow the king's orders. We must fight the temptation and urge to think that we can mount the throne of the king—this is contrary to the substance of the message we proclaim: "Jesus is king." Our motivation is one of grateful obedience, of which we have no control over how the invitees respond. We announce and reannounce the message of the good news of King Jesus as both evangelists and invitees ourselves. The invitation is for us too.

In the parable of the wedding banquet, the king did not blindly repeat his tactics. Instead, the king adjusted his approach after the second set of messengers were mistreated. As evangelists, we must notice what is happening around us and evangelize with wisdom. Evangelists must learn to sense the work of the Holy Spirit in the lives of the people we encounter as we deliver the message of the King. It is to this task we now turn our attention.

CHAPTER 2

The Catalyst of Announcing Jesus: Life

The wind blows wherever it pleases. You hear its
sound, but you cannot tell where it comes from
or where it is going. So it is with everyone
born of the Spirit.
—John 3:8

GOD IS ALWAYS AT WORK, but sometimes we pay
more attention than others. When we're looking,
we notice the Lord's persistent activity. That's why
evangelism often emerges during dynamic life circumstances. Since God is *always* at work, evangelism also emerges in the mundane. God doesn't need
to stir up chaos to convert, but sometimes we need
chaos to stop looking at ourselves and start paying
attention to God. Chaos isn't necessary for God to
work, but it usually helps us to notice God's work.

GOD IS ALWAYS AT WORK

Evangelism can, and should, happen at any time since God is always at work. The converse is also true: we should not expect the Lord to work *more* when people are in critical moments in their lives; this is a human attempt to make God our cosmic evangelistic butler. Yet, people floating on the ever-present current do focus on their navigation more attentively when the water is choppy.

There's a small room in Redmond, Washington where you can't help but pay attention to yourself. In this room, 99.99 percent of sounds are absorbed by special materials on the walls. This room is six hundred times quieter than a peaceful bedroom. Microsoft developed the room to test advanced technology, but the most interesting tests in the room are the ones that happen when humans enter. Most people cannot stay inside this room for more than a few seconds. Those who remain in the room eventually hear the grinding of their joints as they make minor movements, their stomach gurgling, and their heart beating.

We notice our heart thumping after a vigorous workout, a nervous moment, or a visit to the doctor's office. Yet, our heart is always beating. Special circumstances such as a horror movie,

an unexpected drop, or a silent laboratory make us aware of the constant flow of blood running through our veins pumped by our hearts. Stop and notice. Your heart is beating—now, right now. In a moment, your focus will drift off, but your heart-beat will continue.

We read in Lamentations, "The steadfast love of the LORD never ceases, his mercies never come to an end; they are new every morning; great is your faithfulness" (Lam 3:22–23 NRSV). There is never a moment when the Lord's love is not in motion. The Lord's mercy is never-ending. God is continually faithful. God's love, mercy, and faithfulness are within the heartbeat of all creation. This is why the psalmist can write, "It is good to give thanks to the LORD, to sing praises to your name, O Most High; to declare your steadfast love in the morning, and your faithfulness by night" (Ps 92:1–2 NRSV). Anyone at any time can announce God's ever-present love and faithfulness, but we can thank the psalmist for reminding us of this truth. The psalmist quiets the room, positions a stethoscope to listen, looks up to all gathered and says, "Can you hear it? I can. Listen closely with me. God's love and faithfulness are present right here." The evangelist follows in the footsteps of the

psalmist and announces what others can't hear or have forgotten.

Evangelists work in the midst of God's steadfast love for the world. Yet, there is a strange relationship between personal circumstances and our awareness of God's love. I believe that the ups and downs of our lives can serve us in powerful ways to turn to the Lord. I believe this with trembling. I tremble because I fear the downs. I do not want to experience, or re-experience, the low points of my life, even if they might serve to enlighten me to God's love. I'm a fan of the ups. I have attended and supervised many Christian retreats in my life. Inevitably, I run into someone who will say, "I'm not a fan of the 'camp high.' " Fair enough, I get that. But, for me, I'll take *all* the help I can get. I've had enough lows in my life. I'm happy to offset those as much as possible.

How does God use events in our lives to draw us to himself? I believe God's work is more mysterious and unpredictable than we can grasp. What is clear is that *we* tend to link our initial or recurring turning to God with the key events and experiences in our lives.

Fortunately, the Bible provides many accounts of God changing people's lives. These accounts

don't give us all the information we might want about their lives, but we have the information that God wants us to have. We are going to examine three collections of biblical accounts that give snapshots of what people's lives were like when they met Jesus. First, when people encounter Jesus in their daily routines; second, when they find Jesus in the midst of chaos; and third, when they discover Jesus because they are spiritually curious. These accounts will help us to see how God uses events to draw our attention to himself.

Encountering Jesus in Daily Routines

The first collection of accounts are people who were in their normal daily routines just prior to following Jesus. Simon Peter, Andrew, James, and John were fishing before they had an encounter with Jesus that led them to follow him (Matt 4:22; Mark 1:18, 20; Luke 5:11). These men were fishermen, and it is likely that they fished nearly every day. Before meeting Jesus they were doing what they did every day; there was nothing out of the ordinary. We search in vain for riveting details that are common in modern roller coaster testimonials.

We do have one tidbit about that day, but it isn't what we might expect.

When Jesus called Peter, Jesus borrowed his boat to speak, and then Jesus told him to put his nets out again into the seemingly fish-less waters. Then they caught so many fish that the boat began to sink. Peter responded dramatically, but not in the way we might expect. Instead of being eager to follow Jesus, Peter wanted to do the opposite. Peter said, "Go away from me, Lord; I am a sinful man" (Luke 5:8). We might be tempted to read Peter's response through a forced retrospective filter that implies that Peter's words really meant that he was excited and honored to be in the presence of God. We might understand Peter's words as, "You must be the Messiah that we've been waiting for. I am a sinner, please save me." We shouldn't do that. We should take Peter's words at face value. Jesus tells Peter, "Don't be afraid; from now on you will fish for people" (Luke 5:10). Peter's encounter with Jesus left Peter in fear—actual fear, not excitement.

Peter, Andrew, James, and John were going about their normal work routines when Jesus entered their lives. They had nothing leading up to their initial encounter with Jesus that is catalytic to their eventual following of Jesus.

The eventual-apostle Matthew was another person who was simply going about his daily routine prior to following Jesus. Scripture tells us that Matthew was sitting at his tax collector's booth when Jesus approached him (Matt 9:9; Mark 2:14; Luke 5:27). Jesus called Matthew to follow him, and he did. Shortly after that, Matthew hosted Jesus for dinner at his house—what Luke describes as a great banquet (Luke 5:29) attended by his fellow tax collectors (and sinners). We can infer that Matthew's life prior to following Jesus was like many of ours, surrounded by people from his job. It is also safe to say that Matthew must have been financially secure, not only because he had a job as a tax collector but because he had the means to host a great banquet spontaneously. A modern testimonial version of Matthew's story might include the telltale pivot points that we have all come to expect in conversion stories: a man who was financially stable, surrounded by a group of people who were notorious sinners, seeks to do life on his own, and so on. But this is not how Scripture tells Matthew's story. Matthew was simply doing his job and then Jesus saw him. Notice that the initiative in the story—the catalytic moment prior to Matthew's response—was when

Jesus "saw a man named Matthew sitting at the tax collector's booth" (Matt 9:9). Jesus *saw* Matthew— this is the word all three Gospel writers use; the initiative came from Jesus.

It is tempting to read into someone's background the catalyst for following Jesus. But this can't always be the case because everyone has a backstory, but not everyone follows Jesus. We might, in retrospect, weave together parts of our backgrounds to form a narrative that helps us make sense of God's ongoing work in our lives, even prior to following Jesus. Yet, we can't assume that our backgrounds and highs and lows *are* the catalysts for following Jesus because every person has a story with highs and lows, but not all people follow Jesus.

Our background stories are relevant but not always catalytic for following Jesus. This seems to be the case for the Samaritan woman in John 4. We eventually learn, from Jesus, that she had a tumultuous history with husbands who had died and a questionable current relationship with another man. Yet, the real catalyst for her encounter with Jesus was simple: she needed water. Much has been made of the midday hour of *when* she came to the

well, perhaps indicative of her relational status and her Samaritan heritage, but the straightforward reason that she met and responded to Jesus that day was because she was going about her normal routine of getting water at a well. Backstory or not, she, like everyone else, needed water every day—this is what preceded her encounter with Jesus.

Lydia was another woman who was going about her normal routine when she encountered Jesus. Lydia attended a prayer gathering at a river just outside Philippi when Paul spoke to them and "the Lord opened her heart to respond to Paul's message" (Acts 16:14). Lydia had already been a worshiper of God—a gentile who had adopted Jewish belief—so her attendance at a prayer meeting on the Sabbath was a normal routine for her.

Encountering Jesus in Trouble and Chaos

The second collection of accounts of people who began following Jesus are people who were in the midst of obvious troubles and difficulties, physically, emotionally, and spiritually. A large portion of these accounts accompany Jesus's preaching and healing ministry; at times it is difficult to know if

these people followed Jesus out of wild curiosity or genuine faith, though genuine faith and wild curiosity often go together.

Immediately after calling his first disciples, Jesus went through Galilee teaching and healing, so that "large crowds from Galilee, the Decapolis, Jerusalem, Judea and the region across the Jordan followed him" (Matt 4:25). There would have been those who could have said, "I remember the day when it all began. I could hardly believe what I was hearing and seeing, and then it happened to me, my body was healed. That is when I started following Jesus." Then, of course, there were also those that couldn't see anything leading up to following Jesus because they were blind (Matt 20:34; Mark 10:52; Luke 18:43). One moment, they were blind, and the next moment they could see and took their first visible steps right behind the footsteps of Jesus.

A man who had obvious troubles and difficulties, physically, emotionally, and spiritually, was the man known as the Gerasene demoniac (Mark 5:1–20; Luke 8:26–39). The man was demon-possessed, naked, living in tombs, cutting himself with stones, crying out over the tombs and hills, and chains could not hold him—that is, until Jesus *came to him*. Jesus freed him and told him to "return

home and tell how much God has done for you"
(Luke 8:39).

Jesus was brought in place of Barabbas to be
crucified alongside two thieves. Pilate's crucifixion
team played an unlikely role as deliverers of the
good news in the flesh to these condemned men.
This was no normal day for any of them. Each of
the thieves knew they would be crucified and die.
Yet one died with assurance from Jesus that Jesus
would remain with him in life, death, and thereafter. The penitent thief couldn't take a step on his
own as soldiers had nailed his feet to the cross, yet
he knew his next steps would be with Jesus.

Encountering Jesus with
Spiritual Curiosity

People with existing religious curiosity and spiritual questions form the third group of accounts
of people who followed Jesus. Nathanael is one of
these people (John 1:45–51; 21:2). Nathanael was
a serious student of the Scriptures. He was familiar
with the promise of a coming prophet described
in Deuteronomy 18:15 and 18. Jesus chose an allu-
sion Nathanael would understand: Jacob's vision
at Bethel of the angels of God ascending and
descending (Gen 28:12). Nathanael was sitting by

a fig tree—a frequent location for rabbis to discuss Scripture with their students.[10] Prior to meeting and following Jesus, Nathanael studied the
Scriptures and was likely in the midst of his own
questions about the prophet whom Moses said
would arrive. Nathanael's answer arrived when
Jesus *came to him.*

Nicodemus is another person with curiosity and spiritual questions, but unlike Nathanael,
Nicodemus came to Jesus. He came to him with
a loaded statement, saying, "Rabbi, we know that
you are a teacher who has come from God. For
no one could perform the signs you are doing if
God were not with him" (John 3:2). Nicodemus
was a Pharisee and a member of the Sanhedrin,
the Jewish council who met to decide legal matters. He was extremely educated, familiar, and
authoritative in his knowledge of the Scriptures.
What is unusual is that Nicodemus came to Jesus
at night. John records Nicodemus in three episodes
(John 3:1–21; 7:50–52; 19:39–42), which led New
Testament scholar Merrill C. Tenney to call him
"a secret disciple whose faith grew slowly."[11] Later
apocryphal works depict Nicodemus defending
Jesus at his trial, being baptized by Peter and John,
being expelled from the Sanhedrin, and dying a

martyr's death, though these accounts may not be true.[12] Nicodemus came to Jesus with his questions, but as we will see in our discussion of John 3 below, we can hardly attribute God's work in Nicodemus's life to his own volition.

If anyone was ever on a spiritual quest that was interrupted by a life-changing encounter with Jesus, it was Paul. Paul, like Nicodemus, was a Pharisee. Paul was born a Jew, brought up in Jerusalem, and educated in a strict and zealous manner (Acts 22:3). Just before his life-changing encounter with Jesus, Paul was on his way to arrest Christians in Damascus and take them back to Jerusalem as prisoners (Acts 9:2; 22:5; 26:12). This is when Jesus *came to him*. A blazing bright light surrounded Paul and made him fall. Jesus announced, "I am Jesus, whom you are persecuting" (Acts 9:5). In that moment, before Paul got up from the ground, Jesus gave Paul his evangelistic commission:

> Now get up and stand on your feet. I have appeared to you to appoint you as a servant and as a witness of what you have seen and will see of me. I will rescue you from your own people and from

the Gentiles. I am sending you to them
to open their eyes and turn them from
darkness to light, and from the power of
Satan to God, so that they may receive
forgiveness of sins and a place among
those who are sanctified by faith in me.
(Acts 26:16–18)

Paul's misguided and confident religious passion was muted and redirected by a supernatural
encounter with Jesus Christ. Paul found himself on
the ground looking up at Jesus and asking the obvious and proper question for that moment: "Who
are you, Lord?" (Acts 26:15).

Encountering Jesus
and Walking Away

We have seen how people began following Christ
through their normal daily routines, through
emotional, spiritual, and physical struggles, and
through religious curiosity and spiritual questions, but let's look at a fourth type of account, an
account of a man who chose *not* to follow Jesus.

The rich young ruler is a prime example of
someone who heard Jesus's message but did not
take it to heart (Matt 19:16–30; Mark 10:17–30;

Luke 18:18–30). This man asks a question that evangelists dream of: "What good thing must I do to get eternal life?" (Matt 19:16). Jesus answers, "If you want to enter life, keep the commandments" (Matt 19:17). A careful reading shows that Jesus answers a different question, not the one the rich man asked. The rich man asked about how to "get" or "have, hold" eternal life; Jesus answered about how to enter eternal life.

Evangelists can learn from Jesus's careful pastoral redirection. Eternal life is not a token to *hold on to*; it is a life to *enter into*. Even at this point of reading the passage, we might be able to predict the rich man's sad response by the question he asked. The rich man knew how to get things; you "get" rich by possessing the things you seek. Eternal life is not a thing to possess; it is *entrance* into a right relationship with God through spiritual death and resurrection. Jesus never answers his question about how to get or hold eternal life and neither should we, because it is the wrong way to think about salvation. Jesus, instead, explains to the rich man how to enter into eternal life: the man must keep the commandments. Jesus is not preaching a gospel of salvation by works. A friend

of mine wisely suggested that Jesus brought up the second table of the commandments to set up the conversation for the real point of the commandments, the first commandment: "You shall have no other gods before me" (Exod 20:3). The rich man serves a god of money, which he is unwilling to give away, so he walks away from Jesus sad. We know, further, that Jesus is not preaching a gospel of salvation by works because "with man this is impossible, but with God all things are possible" (Matt 19:26).

What were the catalysts that led the rich man to come to Jesus? We do not know. Perhaps the man was already disillusioned by the false promises of being rich (Matt 19:22), or being young (Matt 19:20), or being a ruler (Luke 18:18) with all the power that comes with it. Perhaps the man heard Jesus's earlier teaching about the "eternal fire" and wanted to avoid it (Matt 18:8).[13] Perhaps the man who was an expert at acquiring things sought to acquire the one thing that had evaded his grasp: eternal life. Evangelists who care for souls must listen carefully to what lost people "want" from Jesus. As messengers, we must know the content of the message and not allow it to be confused with something else.

When I was in college, I worked at a vitamin and nutrition store at the now defunct Los Arcos Mall in Scottsdale, Arizona. I was paid minimum wage but also received a small commission when I sold certain products. People came in frequently looking for products to help them lose weight, gain muscle, and to cure aches and pains. Hour after hour, I was confronted by the temptation to make false promises that would take weeks or months to prove or disprove. Each of these promises included many other real-life factors, so no matter what I said, I was in the clear. These promises were never on the labels of these products, of course— that would be illegal and no company wanted to be sued for false advertising. A customer would come in asking me, "Do you have anything to lose weight?" and, without thinking, I would show them certain pills. Over time, I decided to answer their exact question, rather than the inference I made from their question. If a customer asked me, "Do you have anything to lose weight?" I answered, "No. We do not have a product that guarantees weight loss. However, some of our products have been shown to help when combined with proper diet and exercise. I can show you the details here." Customers either appreciated my honesty or they

departed quickly because I simply couldn't provide what they *really* wanted.

Effective Evangelism
Comes from Above

Jesus's conversation with Nicodemus teaches us the real catalyst for effective evangelism. Nicodemus came to Jesus with a statement, not a question. Nicodemus stated that Jesus was a teacher who came from God and that no one could do what Jesus was doing unless God was with him. Jesus, seemingly out of nowhere, redirects their conversation to two topics: the kingdom of God and being born again, or born from above. We will discuss how the kingdom of God fits into the message of evangelism in chapter 4, but for now, notice how being born again requires a catalyst outside of ourselves. If there ever were an activity that included you but you did not initiate, it was your birth. You did not initiate your birth; you can thank your parents for that.

Jesus says an odd thing to Nicodemus: you must be born again. The strangeness of this phrase is lost on many of us because "being born again" is standard Christian jargon for conversion. But notice Nicodemus's response—utter confusion! He

wonders, "How could someone enter the womb again? Look at how big I am, Jesus! I'm not baby-sized anymore!" Jesus clarifies that what he means is "born from above."

Any discussion of being born again, which is a primary focal point of evangelism, must insist that the true catalyst for being a Christian is from above and not from me or from anyone else for that matter, not even the evangelist. For evangelists, like me, this is a difficult pill to swallow. Evangelists have as much control to save people as they did in their own physical birth.

Jesus explains that being born from above is being born of water and the Spirit (John 3:5). Being born of water and the Spirit can be interpreted in many ways;[14] I understand them to form one unified action originating from God in which the water refers to God's cleansing by which God's Spirit is given.[15] All explanations of being born of water and the Spirit require us to admit that both must come from outside of the convert, since the basics of birth are uncontrollable by the individual being born. Only a very confused person would say, "I'm going to birth myself"—it just doesn't make sense. Jesus adds that this birth is like the wind: you can hear its sound but do not know

what direction it came from or where it is going. The catalytic origin for being born from above is the mysterious work of the Holy Spirit.

The great tradition of the church, in its wisdom, has located the work of evangelism as a ministry of the Holy Spirit. The third article of the Nicene Creed teaches us that the Holy Spirit is the "Lord and the Giver of life." Salvation was accomplished by the work of Christ and is applied by the giver of life, the Holy Spirit.

What does this mean for the evangelist? It means that the outcome of evangelism is out of our control. When evangelists care for souls effectively, the outcome is not in our control. I agree with Dale Bruner when he writes, "Every single conversion or return to faith is an absolute, incalculable miracle."[16] If we can't control the Spirit's work of conversion, what then are we to do? Jesus gives us a clue in his words to Nicodemus: listen for the wind.

Our Task: Listen for the Wind

Jesus explained the Spirit's movement as akin to the wind: "You can hear its sound" (John 3:8). What does the Spirit sound like? We are now jumping into deep waters. These waters, like the ocean and

rivers, are full of all sorts of dangers. Returning to the birth metaphor, even the most experienced obstetrician knows the dangers of being too certain about any step along the way and must warn the parents of their uncertainty. Here is some unsolicited medical advice: walk away from any doctor who makes guarantees and be sure to do the same with anyone, even an evangelist or pastor, who makes absolute claims about the movement of the Spirit of God with too much certainty.

While absolute certainty is unlikely, an evangelist with any sensibilities should be alert to how the Holy Spirit might be moving in people with questions like Nicodemus or in the midst of demonic conflict like the man from the Gerasenes. But what about the ho-hum activities of people like Peter and Lydia? As it turns out, the Holy Spirit was on the verge of doing a life-changing work in their lives, but it would have been difficult to predict the Spirit's sudden surge in them.

The wise evangelist should be alert and jump into action when the wind of the Spirit picks up. The key skill is listening. We must listen to God as best we can. We must also listen to people. An underdeveloped skill in many ministers I know is the skill and art of attentive listening. Evangelistic

opportunities often reside in second and third follow-up questions.

Recently I was in a room with a group of four young men. One of them, Travis, made it clear to the others that he was not a Christian. The other three guys pummeled Travis with confrontational apologetics questions for about a half hour. Travis graciously and kindly replied to each of their questions. The conversation went nowhere.

The following day I asked Travis if he wanted to meet up. After catching up, I told him that I admired his patience and the kindness that I observed in him the previous day. I asked him where he learned to be so patient and kind in those types of conversations. He told me about his closest friends. His friends have many different beliefs about God, and he respected them for that. I asked him what he had learned from his friends about God.

For the next hour, I practiced genuine curiosity and asked quality follow-up questions. It might surprise you, but the leading skill of *announcing* the good news is not an announcement; evangelistic care of souls begins with *listening*. Our conversation felt a bit like bushwhacking through a thick jungle forest, not knowing where I was going. Such

is the way of the Spirit most of the time. I didn't bring an agenda to convert Travis, and, in fact, he didn't accept Jesus that day. Instead, I went on a bit of a Holy Spirit search, listening carefully to see what the Holy Spirit might be doing in Travis's world. The primary tool I used in my search was my ears. Along the way, I silently asked the Holy Spirit to give me the right words to say and questions to ask Travis. At the end it seemed natural to ask Travis if I could pray for him. He agreed, and so I did. That's the end. I have no further updates. I don't know what God has done with these seed conversations. Most, if not all, of my evangelistic conversations go something like this. Asking natural and organic questions, and follow-up questions, is like ripping some grass from the ground and throwing it up in the air to gauge the direction of the wind.

The Patient Reality of Evangelism

I want to warn you against two tempting evangelistic tactics: overzealousness and pragmatism. Eager evangelists must avoid becoming evangelistic ambulance chasers. Wise pastors and ministers eventually learn to bite their tongues when sitting with someone who is suffering. It is rare that

a person in the midst of pain or tragedy needs a bold (and foolish) attempt to explain or minimize the situation. Usually the best tactics are sitting in silence and simply being present, or offering a word from Scripture, defaulting to Jesus's experience or the words of the psalmists. Wise evangelists will likewise resist the urge to resolve a painful moment by directing the unconverted sufferer to put their faith in God for the first time. It could be the right moment, but please don't assume that it is a better moment than other moments. In fact, there are good reasons to practice evangelistic restraint in those moments.

I waited a long time to tell my high school sweetheart, and eventual wife, Erin, that I love her. I had felt that I loved her for a long time, but I knew that when I spoke those words to her for the first time, I never wanted to retract them—ever. So, I decided that I would tell her those words not in a moment of high emotion, but on a typical day. She and I remember that day and moment in all its detail. I realize my approach isn't the most romantic, but for me the primary meaning of the love I wanted to give Erin wasn't romance—that was a part of it but not the most important part. Another way to put it is that I wanted to be

sober-minded in my first confession of love to my eventual wife. I wanted it to be a moment when I had all my wits about me and full clarity in what I meant by the words "I love you." Decades later, I've said those words in moments that were full of excitement and emotion but also in moments of difficulty and sadness.

A second tempting evangelistic tactic is to exaggerate, oversimplify, or even lie about God's saving work. We might call this our testimony. Evangelicals likely identify with this tactic more than other traditions, but this temptation finds its way into many faith stories. Conversion testimonies follow a predictable format: first, I was facing something difficult in my life; second, I put my faith in Christ; finally, things are better now. I used to tell my own story this way and taught others to do the same.

For a season of my life, I coached and orchestrated people in an evangelistic illustration called "cardboard testimonies." In this illustration, a person would walk on stage with a piece of cardboard to show the audience and then flip it over before walking off stage. Written on the first side of the sign would be something like "Lost, sinful, hurt," and the second side would read, "Healed

by the love of Christ." For many people this story could be the truth of exactly what happened. Yet, there are many obvious risks in assigning this narrative.

This narrative is the formula of pragmatism and consumerism. The gospel does not promise to make our lives better. In this narrative Christ becomes simply an option in a formula that can be replaced by almost anything that makes things better. When this narrative is told, it suggests that Christianity comes mostly to people in crisis. Further, this narrative cuts off our stories and God's work, limiting it to a short period of our lives. Wise evangelism will highlight God's lifelong work in our lives.

God is always at work. The steadfast love of the Lord never ceases; his mercies never come to an end. God directed his steadfast love toward us before any memorable difficulties happened in our lives. God showered us with his mercy when we didn't turn to the Lord. God's love and mercy continue in our lives like the nearly silent sound of the blood rushing through our body right now. The catalysts for evangelism don't hinge on significant moments in our lives. The best catalyst for evangelism, and a trustworthy method for evangelists,

is to help God's chosen people to listen carefully to the silent sound of the wind of the Holy Spirit that constantly swirls around us all. This pastoral skill develops over time for those who listen and look for it, but developing this skill does not guarantee evangelistic success. As it turns out, we have no control over how the gospel will land with those whom we deliver it to.

The Context of Announcing Jesus: Christians

Let us not become weary in doing good, for at the proper time we will reap a harvest if we do not give up. Therefore, as we have opportunity, let us do good to all people, especially to those who belong to the family of believers.
—Galatians 6:9–10

I DO NOT HAVE A GREEN THUMB. WhaTEVER the opposite of green is, that is the color of my thumb. My neighbor Brian has a beautiful and flourishing yard. He owns a landscaping company, and his thumb is evergreen, much to my envy. The worst part of my lawn right now, and for many of

us in Phoenix, is the grass. Keeping a healthy lawn is notoriously difficult in Phoenix due to the hellish heat. People who move to Phoenix are surprised to learn that you have to keep two lawns every year: a winter lawn and a summer lawn. When the temperature rises above 100°F it kills the winter lawn. Fortunately, the summer grass goes dormant in the winter and rises from its slumber around this time as long as it is watered and fertilized. When winter approaches, the summer grass goes dormant again, and, if you do nothing, you will have no grass in the winter because the summer heat obliterated the previous year's winter grass. So every year people in Phoenix make their trek to Home Depot to buy the seed and fertilizer for their winter lawn.

Our first home had a small and manageable lawn, but when we moved to our current home, with a much larger lawn, I had to upgrade my tools—this is when I bought the Scotts Turf Builder 23lb Broadcast Spreader. This product is equipped with Scotts's exclusive EdgeGuard Technology, which allows you to spread your seed accurately. You can even control the panel's precision rate setting to deliver accurate coverage up to five thousand square feet. The Scotts Turf Builder

Spreader comes calibrated and ready to use, so you can get started right away. You would think that this product guarantees a yard that would make Brian jealous. Nope. As it turns out, a flourishing winter lawn in Phoenix requires much more than slinging seeds. But, every winter, my optimism returns.

After cutting down the summer lawn as low as possible—we call this "scalping the lawn"—Brian reminds me to water my lawn to prepare the soil. So far, so good. Then, I load my Scotts Turf Builder with twenty-three pounds of top-notch seed and start to push the spreader around my yard. This is when I face several tactical decisions. The easy part is making the circuitous route through my yard several times until I spread all the seed evenly. The tricky part is my use of the EdgeGuard feature on my spreader. The EdgeGuard is a plastic guard engaged when spreading seed near the edge of the lawn so seed isn't flung onto the gravel or patio. One side of my yard winds back and forth like a wave, and I'm never sure how to ensure that seed will land on the lawn but not all over the gravel. If I play it too safe, I end up with dirt patches in my lawn because no seed was placed there, but if I overdo it, then I end up with seed in my gravel,

and as my luck would have it, that seed always flourishes more than my actual lawn, just to mock me. Yes, my lawn mocks me. Brian is probably behind all of this.

My failures as a lawn owner are many. Brian's lawn always turns out great, mine doesn't. We use the same seed, fertilizer, and watering schedule. Brian helps me with all of this. After a decade of failures, there is only one explanation: my problem is user error—me. The problem is not the fertilizer, nor the seed. The problem is me.

The Task of Delivering

Modern attitudes toward evangelism gravitate toward pragmatism. This is a problem. The primary problem is the assumption that the primary goal of evangelism is winning souls, or, perhaps, when we are a bit more thoughtful, making disciples. These are noble desires, but ones that we are unable to control. To return to my story, we think evangelism is like a lawn; if it is healthy, we must have done something right, and if it is full of weeds and patches of dirt, we botched it. Passersby envy Brian's lawn and feel pity for mine because the results are clear and obvious: Brian has it figured out and I failed. Evangelism too often devolves

into an amateurish empirical social science that Christians and churches eagerly take onboard because they are counting the wrong thing. The core of evangelism is being a messenger. The message is not ours, and the effectiveness of the message is not ours.

Who are the top ten mail carriers in your state? You don't know because it's not something we take note of. I'm not trying to disparage the fine folks who deliver the mail, but the primary job of a mail carrier is to take someone else's message and deliver it to the intended recipient. Either the mail reaches its destination or it doesn't. When my son opened an envelope and inside was a generous graduation gift (much more than he expected), my son did not track down our mailman—as wonderful as he is. No, my son contacted the sender, not the deliverer of the gift.

In modern evangelism we celebrate, study, and idolize far too many *messengers* while minimizing the *sender*. We confuse the importance of the message with the messenger. This is a manifestation of worshiping the creation rather than the creator, of which Paul warned the church in Rome (Rom 1:25). Paul knew the temptation of worshiping the messenger above the sender, and he rebuked the

Corinthians for this. Paul wrote, "What I mean is this: One of you says, 'I follow Paul'; another, 'I follow Apollos'; another, 'I follow Cephas'; still another, 'I follow Christ.' Is Christ divided? Was Paul crucified for you? Were you baptized in the name of Paul?" (1 Cor 1:12–13). Unfortunately, too many people have been evangelized in names other than the Lord Jesus Christ. They have been baptized in the name of their church, parachurch, or pastor rather than being baptized in the name of the Lord Jesus Christ.

Last month I was on my way to meet someone for coffee while driving next to a Ferrari. A few minutes later, we both arrived at the same coffee shop. I got out of my Honda. The Ferrari owner got out of his car. Cars are nice, but the most important aspect of a car is getting the contents from point A to point B. If the car can't get people from point A to point B, it is worthless, whether it is fancy or plain. Cars exist to transport humans. Evangelists exist to transport the gospel. Some evangelists are fancy, others aren't. The only question that matters is if the gospel is delivered *from* the word of God *to* humans.

So, the messenger matters, but only because of the message. The messenger delivers the message

from its source to its recipients. The next chapter will discuss the content of the message, but for now let's explore a parable Jesus gave us that highlights the role of the messenger and its recipients.

Unlimited Delivery

The parable of the sower (Matt 13:1–23; Mark 4:1–20; Luke 8:4–15) wouldn't exist without the sower who sows the seed, but the bulk of this parable is about the four soils. While Jesus calls the parable the "parable of the sower" (Matt 13:18), it could also be called the parable of the soils. The target, the indirect object, of Jesus's explanation in Matthew's account is "anyone [who] hears the message" (Matt 13:19). Evangelists have another reason to call it the parable of the soils because we should think about the *people* we are evangelizing, not just the ones who are doing the evangelizing.

This parable says little about the seed itself, about the content of the message that is heard. The parable assumes that the seed is the same for each of the four soils. The seed, which we explore in chapter 4, is the word of God (Luke 8:11). The parable follows a three-part form in all three Gospels: the parable, a reference to Isaiah 6, and the explanation. I want to explore these through the lens of

the sower: this is the person who is the messenger, the evangelist of the gospel.

It might surprise us that the sower casts seeds upon all four soil types. Wouldn't we expect a farmer to take better care casting his seeds rather than throwing so they might end up in soil with thorns or among rocks or, especially, near a path? In the parable, does Jesus want his hearers to assume that the scattering is unwise, inexperienced, or irresponsible, especially with such precious seed as the word of God? No. When I read the parable, I think back to my own lawn and how I would rather have some seed be spread into my gravel rather than have good soil left with bare patches all winter long. This is a lesson for the evangelist; it is better to spread the word of God liberally—and as we will see later, regularly—than to be stingy.

Notice too that each of the soils hears the message: the path people hear the message (Matt 13:18; Mark 4:15; Luke 8:12); the rocky ground people hear the message (Matt 13:20; Mark 4:16; Luke 8:13); the thorny soil people hear the message (Matt 13:22; Mark 4:18; Luke 13:14); and the good soil people hear the message (Matt 13:23; Mark 4:20; Luke 8:15). All four cases are examples of faithful evangelism. Evangelists can

only control getting the message from point A to point B. Like a car, our job is to deliver the passenger, which is the word of God. This is tough news to swallow for many evangelists because we often feel like a successful or lousy evangelist based upon what happens *after* we drop off the word—though delivery and reception of the word is never a one-time event, as we will discuss further in chapter 7.

Accepting Delivery

After evangelists deliver the word and the people hear, we might find out the condition of the soil or we might not. Jesus teaches that the seed cast on the path is *heard* but is not *understood* (Matt 13:19). Satan is also at work (Matt 13:19; Mark 4:15; Luke 8:12). The devil's plans are undeterred, unaffected, and remain no matter how well, or poorly, the word is delivered. This is one reason why being an evangelist is so difficult. The devil takes the word away from the hearers' hearts "so that they may not believe and be saved" (Luke 8:12). In evangelism, as in all things, there is more than meets the eye. Thus, evangelistic strategies based solely upon mere effectiveness or pragmatism fail to account for the work of Satan.

We might not know the true condition of the soil because faith germination and growth are slow processes. My wife and I made a deal with our kids that we would get a dog if they could prove themselves with stepping-stone animal commitments. Our children sought to prove themselves with their new friend Alfonzo the hermit crab. We had no idea that hermit crabs, while very simple creatures, are also incredibly difficult to nurture. My kids were extremely committed to Alfonzo's flourishing. They read books, websites, and consulted fellow hermit crab owners to ensure success. The biggest challenge is that hermit crabs are ... hermits. You can't really tell when they are awake or even if they are alive. Alfonzo buried himself deep in our sandy terrarium for weeks at a time, emerging seemingly at random. Each time Alfonzo went missing, my daughter Lilly hoped for the best but often expected the worst. One day, Alfonzo was up to his usual business. We hadn't seen him in weeks. The experts we consulted warned us not to disturb our hermit crab if he was burrowed and hidden away. Our interference could hurt his health or even kill him. I told Lilly that we should dig around a little because we hadn't seen Alfonzo in over a month. Lilly gave me a stern look and slowly shook

her head back and forth. No words were needed. We left Alfonzo alone. About a month later, I asked again since Alfonzo was nowhere to be seen. After three months, Lilly agreed, and we discovered that Alfonzo was dead. We didn't know what was happening beneath the surface. This is often the case with people who hear the word of God. Usually time will tell. But unlike hermit crabs, humans shouldn't be left alone after their initial evangelistic hearing of the word of God. Caring for souls evangelistically is a not a one-time endeavor.

People who fall away quickly from their faith appear to be the rocky soil. These people hear the word of God, spring up quickly and receive it with joy, but only remain in the faith for a short time. The parable teaches that trouble, persecution, and times of testing reveal the shallowness of this soil. I have seen this sad cycle repeat many times as an evangelist. The evangelistic approaches I tend to employ are relational. Because of this, my friendships weave together with the gospel tightly. When non-Christian people hear the gospel and respond in this environment, it can be difficult to discern authentic Christian response from social conformity. I have learned to avoid trying to guess who is authentic or who is just placating the crowd, or

some combination of both, because my task is delivery, not reception. The task God gives us is to plant and water; we can't control growth (1 Cor 3:6).

One of the many failures of my lawn care is that I overwater. In my eagerness to have a thick and flourishing lawn, my ignorance leads me to an oversimplistic maintenance method: the more water, the better. I know this tactic doesn't work. I should have learned this lesson through a decade of failure and constant reminders from my landscaping-genius neighbor Brian. The best watering schedules require wisdom, experience, and a keen eye for the weather and conditions. It is tempting to read Luke's account of the rocky soil and to fall into my error. Luke writes, "The plants withered because they had no moisture" (Luke 8:6). The naïve response to a withering plant is overwatering; if the plant is withering because there is no moisture, then just add water! Water isn't the only issue. The issue is the soil; it is full of rocks. Yes, the plant withers because it lacks moisture, but the reason there is no moisture is because water *can't* be retained in rocks. But can the soil be changed? More on that in a moment.

When I see people who receive the word of God and endure for a while but begin to fall away,

my instinct is to overwater them with everything in my evangelistic and pastoral tool belt: prayer, the word of God, church engagement, sacraments, and more. I rally the firefighters to unwind the fire hose. These are the good tools, and wisdom is needed at the pump to adjust the evangelistic and pastoral dials—more isn't always better—but the issue might be beyond treatment; the issue may be rocky soil. One of my most disheartening and discouraging experiences is to see a recent convert whither and fade away. Most importantly, it saddens me to see someone lack a genuine and healthy connection to the Lord. Additionally, I can't help but feel guilty. I wish I could say that isn't true, but it is. I *know* that I am not in control of someone else's spiritual growth—only God makes things grow—however, I simply can't shake how it feels to watch someone wither and fade away. It is painful to watch, but at least it is over quickly in the case of rocky soil. That's not always the case.

The thorny soil chokes out the growing seed slowly. These people hear the word of God, but the worries of life and the deceitfulness of wealth makes it unfruitful. This plant keeps growing but without fruit. When my family and I moved into our house, we planted a lemon tree in our backyard.

Citrus trees grow easily in Phoenix, unlike lawns. Our lemon tree had everything it needed: plenty of sun, a drip system delivering water each morning, and occasional citrus tree fertilizer. All we needed to do was give it time to grow, and it did. Each year, little by little, it sprouted branches, the trunk thickened, and the leaves became fuller. But it lacked one key thing: lemons. I learned that it could take two to three years for fruit to arrive on a young tree, but after six years of a healthy lemon tree without lemons, I was concerned. Fortunately, in year seven, three scrawny lemons emerged, and in the next season, we were able to make tasty lemonade. Today, we have more lemons than we need. We give them to friends and neighbors. I'm glad we didn't grab a shovel, dig up our lemon tree, and throw it in the dumpster. We just needed to be patient.

As an evangelist, I've learned similar patience. When I see folks who don't fall away from their faith but appear to have little or no growth in love, joy, peace, patience, kindness, goodness, faithfulness, gentleness, or self-control, it alarms me. I double-check their spiritual support system. But I have also learned to be patient—a fruitful harvest might be coming. We need to be careful and

humble to know with certainty, but Jesus teaches us that slow growth may be due to the thorny deception of worry, wealth, and desire for things other than the Lord. Fruitlessness appears to be a product of its support system. Worry often arises from giving our circumstances access to our heart. The deceitfulness of wealth causes us to turn our leaves toward darkness rather than light. The desire for other things poisons our root system. To borrow a phrase from James K. A. Smith, you are what you love; similarly, you are what you eat. When you feed yourself worry, greed, and envy, your fruit can appear rotten. This isn't a book about discipleship, this is a book about evangelism, but, as we will discuss further in chapter 6, we should not divide evangelism and discipleship. Evangelists who lack long-term vision often steer the ship in the wrong direction.

Good soil produces a crop—the promise sounds too good to be true—one hundred, sixty, or thirty times what was sown. It's true. I've seen it. But we need to clarify what we *count* as fruit. Evangelists might rush to imagine evangelistic fruit as the multiplication of Christians: more people being saved. A good-soil person who becomes a Christian might evangelize others and see thirty,

sixty, or one hundred more people come to faith, who in turn will do the same, yielding exponential results and the evangelization of the entire world. I hope and pray for this to happen, but I also want to warn you to think beyond counting people. We shouldn't rush to count people as fruit.

A temptation for pastors is to measure their ministries by "butts, bricks, and budgets." The number of "butts" at church, "bricks" for new buildings, and "budgets" that are healthy. These features are tempting because they are quantifiable; you can *count* those things. The fruit of the Spirit are rarely quantifiable. Evangelists face a similar temptation when we read the parable of the soils. We default to imagining thirty, sixty, or one hundred more *converts* because fruit is the natural metaphor that fits the parable and, temptingly, you *can* count fruit that grows on trees. One orange, two oranges, and so on. Spiritual fruit is not as easy to count as oranges. What would happen if evangelists added another metric to their examinations and calibrated fruitfulness to increased love, joy, peace, patience, kindness, goodness, faithfulness, gentleness, and self-control thirty, sixty, or one hundred times over? All this could emerge from just one Spirit-filled person; you could probably

imagine right now a person you know that seems to have this type of overabundant Christ-like aroma. I think of my friend Grace. The Holy Spirit and the aroma of Christ fills the room when she walks in. I hope you know people like Grace.

The good-soil person is a person who, like the others, hears the word, but then also "understands" it, "accepts" it, and "retains" it (Matt 13:23; Mark 4:20; Luke 8:15). While we can't control or even know the soil type of another person, we can look for external indicators of what might be happening below the surface. Jesus gives us these guides, of which we would be wise to align our proclamation. When we announce and reannounce the gospel, as we will discuss further in chapter 6, we should not only aim for people to hear the gospel; we need to check to see if people *understand* the gospel, *accept* the gospel, and *retain* the gospel. Another word for this is catechesis, which is useful for both the initial and ongoing proclamation of the gospel. Calvin urges, "We ought to be extremely careful, that the fruit of the Gospel be not lost through our negligence."[17] Evangelists have a responsibility to God to deliver the announcement and reannouncement of the good news, of the word of God, in a way that it will be rightly received. Caring for souls

evangelistically is a skill that is learned. A good mail carrier delivers a letter right up to the doorstep, or even better, hands it to the person directly.

Modern evangelistic approaches, especially those among evangelicals, end up stumbling backward into the great tradition's ongoing practice of catechism whether they know it or not. Early evangelicals such as George Whitefield and John Wesley found the need to create ongoing localized societies in the wake of their preaching in order to water and grow baby seeds of faith. Modern evangelists such as Billy Graham learned to partner with local churches and create follow-up materials for similar reasons. Since spiritual rebirth is a miracle from above, it can happen in an instant. Spiritual fruit takes time to appear and usually emerges when the word of God is rightly understood, accepted, and retained.

BROKEN EARS

I was at a large family gathering recently and the center of attention was so small you could easily miss her. The center of attention was a furry puppy named Trixie. The entire family commented endlessly about "Trixie this" and "Trixie that." Everyone adored Trixie, except me—remember,

I'm the one who forced my daughters to endure the Alfonzo experiment. My daughters spent several years winning me over before we finally visited our local animal rescue shelter and adopted a mutt we named after our wonderful Scottish friend Euan. I'll admit, I'm glad we have Euan. But I was certain we didn't need Trixie. One dog is enough for me. Yet, my daughters were up to their old tricks. "Trixie is so soft," "Look at her little furry legs, so cute!" "Euan would love to have a friend like Trixie!" they commented with veteran precision. My eyes glossed over. My ears tuned out their arguments. My heart was far from finding a place for Trixie. My daughters employed ingenious evangelistic efforts for the sake of all things canine, but despite their best efforts, the outcome was already certain. My daughters knew this too, but their determination is off the charts. Who knows? Maybe by the time you read these words, I will be eating mine and buying more dog food.

Jesus weaves in a difficult and relevant teaching between his parable of the soils and his explanation of the parable. Bible readers might wonder why Jesus included this passage; at first glance, it doesn't seem necessary. The overall section might read easier and more expectedly as two parts

(parable and explanation of parable). Instead, Jesus introduces the words the Lord gave to the prophet Isaiah. These words hold a lesson for us.

The primary senses the messenger evangelist engages are hearing and seeing. You can usually see and hear an evangelist. Imagine for a moment if you could neither see nor hear. Close your eyes, plug your ears. Evangelism becomes quite difficult, if not practically impossible utilizing normal techniques without seeing and hearing. I'm proud and fortunate to work with an inspiring group of Christians that minister and evangelize people with disabilities. My friends have taught me thoughtful and innovative ways to communicate the good news to people with differing abilities. I have seen them share the good news with people who cannot see and hear. It is not only possible, it happens every day. While it is possible to evangelize people who cannot see and hear, Jesus is not speaking about photons and sound waves; he is speaking about the mysterious communication of God that arrives through determination of the Holy Spirit.

One of the most painful and disheartening experiences I endure as an evangelist is seeing people reject the good news of Jesus Christ. When

people reject the gospel, it simply does not make sense to me. It pains me because I *can* see. I can see the treasure hidden in the field, but they can't. I grasp the value of the pearl of great price, but they don't. Jesus explained the benefit of seeing and grasping this treasure: "I [the LORD] would heal them" (Matt 13:15) that "they might turn and be forgiven!" (Mark 4:12). Calvin explains it this way, "The lively word of God, at the hearing of which the whole world ought to tremble, strikes their ears to no purpose, and without any advantage."[18] When I see and hear the gospel, I want to reach out and grab it for myself immediately while some of my friends look the other way and for something else. Fredrick Buechner's definition of the word "lust" parallels this ignorance, he writes, "Lust is the craving for salt of a man who is dying of thirst."[19] My friends who reject the gospel hold their breath and suffocate inside a room of life-giving oxygen. But why?

Not only does the rejection of the gospel not make intellectual sense to me, but it is an adulterous betrayal of the most intimate love ever given, the love of God. Their rejection crushes my soul. The pain of observing people reject the gospel seeps into my endless personal insecurities. Since

I can't understand why people would reject the gospel, I conclude that *I* must be the problem. Rejection is only understandable because of every shortcoming I have, real and imagined. I have a difficult time putting into words how real this pain is, how difficult it is to shake gospel-rejection off my conscience.

When I am sober-minded about the reality of the evangelistic task, I remember that as an evangelist my task is to deliver the good news. I am not responsible for reception or response. People dodge certified letters and pretend not to be home. A proposal can be rejected. Alternatively, when the letter is received and accepted, the mail carrier isn't the person to thank. Calvin writes that it is as if the Lord tells us, "You will indeed teach without any good effect; but do not regret your teaching, for I enjoin it upon you; and do not refrain from teaching, because it yields no advantage; only obey me, and leave to my disposal all the consequences of your labors."[20] The task of the evangelist is to obey God.

Why does Jesus include the Lord's words to Isaiah during his discussion and explanation of the variety of responses to the gospel? It is because we can't change the soil. God already knows the soil and still asks us to spread the seed widely. To

make his point, Jesus reminds us of what the Lord asked Isaiah to do. Isaiah might be remembered as a prophet, but he should also be thought of as an evangelist, a deliverer of news. The news was good for those who would repent; the news was bad for those who wouldn't.

Jesus references Isaiah 6, where God called, cleansed, commissioned, and gave Isaiah a message to share with Israel. The Lord asked, "Who will go for us?" and Isaiah responded, "Here am I. Send me!" (Isa 6:8). Many evangelists have responded similarly to the Lord's call. Many people, and lectionaries, end their reading at verse 8, perhaps because the next passage is so difficult. It begins on a promising note: the Lord says, "Go and tell this people ..." If we were to stop there and not know the next words, we might pause and think, "Here it comes, this is ideal. God is giving me the exact words the people need to hear. I will repeat whatever I hear next. What is it that you want me to say?" But then we read the next words: "Be ever hearing, but never understanding" (Isa 6:9). We might think, "Wait, this can't be right. Why would God explicitly command me to 'tell' a message they will hear and 'never understand'?" These people will see, but not perceive. The Lord said, "Make

the heart of this people calloused; make their ears
dull and close their eyes" (Isa 6:10). The words the
Lord gave Isaiah were meant to contribute toward
the callousing of their hearts, the dulling of their
ears, and the closing of their eyes.

Delivering a message of importance that is
likely to be rejected creates ethical questions for
the evangelist. It can feel as if delivering the message of the good news does more harm than good.
Paul explained that to some people his preaching
will be "a sweet smell" but to others it brings "death
to you" (2 Cor 2:15–16). Calvin is right when he
says, "Ungodly men have no right to blame the
word for making them worse after having heard it.
The whole blame lies on themselves in altogether
refusing it admission."[21] Again, you can't blame the
messenger for the message; the issue is between
the author and the recipient.

Years ago, the parents and administration of a
Christian school asked me to establish an evangelistic ministry for the students. They recognized
that many of the students were not Christians and
that the ministries of the school, as strong as they
were, weren't having the effect they'd hoped. As I
learned more about the students and their environment, I stumbled across a word that seemed to fit

their situation: inoculation. The way inoculation works, as best as I understand it, is to give a very small and controllable dose of a virus to a subject to build up defense mechanisms against the virus. More so than evangelizing at public schools, this was my experience at the Christian school: sharing the gospel was met with unusual resistance. But the resistance I encountered with the non-Christian students at the Christian school included a lot of smiles, head nods, and polite engagement. Our evangelistic efforts were killed by kindness.

Resolute Delivery

Real-life opposition to evangelism, in my modern American suburban experience, is more often met with vague kindness and general muted disinterest than what I read in the oft-repeated accounts from church history and today's saucy social media posts. Modern Christian evangelism is a snoozer. The gospel message has become mundane, unspectacular, and difficult to notice in our culture. This is the way calluses form; this is the way ears dull; this is the way eyes close. These body parts stop working over time. Seemingly healthy hearts callous until they are hard as stone and die. Efficient

ears attenuate until they register nothing. Sharp eyes go from blurry to blind. Patients may be able to pinpoint key debilitating moments—a heart that undergoes a stressful season, an explosion too close to an ear, an eye that fails because it got poked. As much as a rocky-soil person could say that their rocks are due to the hypocrisy of Christians (modern or ancient), or intellectual roadblocks, or any other excuse, this isn't the real reason. Jesus includes this passage from Isaiah in the middle of the parable of the soils so that the seed spreader, the evangelist, stays true to the prophetic call to deliver God's word no matter what the response is of the recipients.

There are three people in this story we need to consider to understand the parable fully. At first, it might seem like there are only two: the sower and the soil-people. But there is another person in the story that is required to make sense of the story: the creator. Thus, the three people are: the creator, the sower, and the soil-people. Framing the parable this way makes better sense of the task of the evangelist because the sower is the middle person between God and his people. The enduring connection comes through the seed, not the sower. The sower plays a temporary and intermediary

role. The enduring connection between God and God's people comes through the word of God via the power of the Spirit, not through the temporary work of the evangelist (or the pastor). Paul's words in his second letter to the Corinthians further highlight the critical and intermediary role of the evangelist as a messenger of the word of God.

Paul explains that God gave Christians the "ministry of reconciliation" (2 Cor 5:18). It is enormously tempting, again, to misunderstand our role in the ministry of reconciliation. Put bluntly: we do not "do" the reconciling of people to God. This is clear in verse 19, when Paul shows who does the reconciling. Paul writes, "God was reconciling us to himself through Christ." We must understand the relationship between the "ministry of reconciliation," of which God gave Christians, and God "reconciling us to himself." The evangelist must understand the role as a *messenger* and *not the author* of the message of reconciliation. Paul makes this distinction explicit near the end of verse 19 when he writes that God "committed to us the message of reconciliation." Ministry *is* the delivery of the message. Ministry *is not* the act of reconciling. Paul continues his explanation that God makes "his appeal through us." The appeal

to "be reconciled to God" (2 Cor 5:20) is God's appeal, not ours. Evangelists are not brokers of a salvation deal. Evangelists do not get a 3 percent commission, like realtors, when people settle into their new place of eternal life. You can spot this mentality when ministries and evangelists try to prove their worth by providing statistics regarding conversions or how many people "met Christ."

God uses Christians as the normal means to communicate the good news of the gospel. There are two temptations facing the evangelist as they carry out their essential task, which is announcing God's good news. The primary temptation is to think that they are the author of the good news. The secondary temptation is to think that acceptance or denial of the good news by the recipients is due to their delivery. And yet, the evangelist is *not* neutral in evangelism. The evangelist is necessary for evangelism. Paul writes, "How, then, can they call on the one they have not believed in? And how can they believe in the one of whom they have not heard? And how can they hear without someone preaching to them?" (Rom 10:14). This important task requires great patience, but the evangelist only has a task because there is an urgent message to deliver.

CHAPTER 4

The Content of Announcing Jesus: The Word of God

*Pray also for me, that whenever I speak,
words may be given me so that I will fearlessly
make known the mystery of the gospel.*
—Ephesians 6:19

As I peered over the edge of my Bible, I saw a dozen faces looking right back at me clinging to whatever I said next. I trembled.

I came to faith in high school at a large weekend camp retreat. I didn't grow up going to church, and prior to my conversion I knew little or nothing about religion or Christianity. After I became a Christian, I was thankful that my friends and

leaders guided me to a strong church. I began attending youth group every Wednesday and church every Sunday. Soon, I was baptized and began serving in my church. My service at the church included simple things like setting up chairs, doing announcements at youth group, and playing in the worship band. My leaders trained me to do outreach ministry at the junior high school I had attended.

The outreach ministry was a ton of fun. We connected with students by spending a lot of time with them. I became their basketball coach, we played golf together, and we spent evenings lingering at the Pizza Hut all-you-can-eat buffet. After about a year of building these relationships and outreach meetings, we had all become close friends. By then, I was a freshman in college, and they were eighth-graders in junior high. These young men really looked up to me, and I had a huge amount of influence on their lives. I increasingly recognized the responsibility I had to be a good example and that when I opened my mouth, they were listening *carefully*—which sounds strange when you think of junior high boys, but trust me, they listen more than it might appear.

Later that year, the leaders of our outreach group asked me to give my first talk, a mini sermon at the end of our meeting. I was terribly anxious and excited in equal measure. I admired many of the speakers in our outreach group. They struck me as clever, funny, and insightful, all while communicating the truth about Jesus. Most of all, I thought back to the speaker who spoke when I came to faith. I was overwhelmed by the opportunity to share a similar message, even if it was on a much smaller scale. That is when I freaked out.

I trembled as my eyes looked beyond the pages of my Bible because I realized that "my guys" would believe anything that I told them about Jesus. Like lemmings, my junior-high friends would trust *my words about God*—this was no small thing. Some people say that the number one fear humans have is the fear of public speaking; in that moment, and in almost all similar opportunities that have followed, my number one fear is the fear of twisting or misrepresenting the word of God. Like many people, I face all the normal temptations in those moments. I ask, "Will they like me?" "Was I clear?" and "Did I say something dumb?" But I couldn't

shake the pivotal role I have as an evangelist to deliver God's word to others for the first time. I wondered if my words would be the right words, or maybe more importantly, true words.

THE BEACH IS THAT WAY

Being an evangelist can feel like a local giving directions to a new person in town. The new person really has no idea where they are or where they are going, but they have a sense of where they want to be. The key moment for the local is when they stick out their arm, point their finger, and say, "Go *that* way." When my family and I were in Scotland for my graduate and doctoral work, we frequently provided directions to tourists. Because I tend to second-guess myself, later in the day I wondered frequently, "Did that person get to their destination?" I rarely reencountered the stranger to confirm if my directions worked, adding to my tendency to second-guess myself. What I learned is to only give directions to destinations that I knew well.

I would be a fool to show up in a new town and give directions to people. I would equally be a fool to be a local in town and give directions to a place I had not been to personally. My initial time

in Scotland lacked a tool that would have made this task much simpler: a smartphone. We used to have a similar tool: a map (remember how hard those were to fold?). Modern smartphones now come equipped with a digital compass to help us to stick out our arm, point our finger, and say confidently, "Go *that* way." The word of God equips us for this task in evangelism. We cannot rely merely on our experience, intuition, or best guess.

When I got back to my car after my short talk to my thirteen-year-old friends, I made a lifelong commitment to make the focal point of my speaking and evangelism the word of God. I want to point people in the right direction, with great confidence, and with, Lord-willing, as little second-guessing of myself as possible.

Be Clear, the Direction Is Jesus

The content of the good news is the word of God. The word of God is not the word of "me," it is not the word of "you," it is not the word of "our church," it is not the word of "self-improvement." The word of God is preeminently the word of the good news of Jesus Christ. There are endless temptations to make the news of evangelism a message that will point people in the wrong destination.

Evangelistic debris is scattered throughout retrospective personal salvation testimonies. Remember, evangelism and being born again are works of the Holy Spirit. Discussions of what happened in a person's faith are holy ground because they attempt to retrace the mysterious work of the Spirit. There is a gentle and expanding trail of waves behind the boat that gives a faint outline of its previous path, but those waves fade quickly and combine with others to blur its true origin. Yet, the blurred path still provides general contours. This is why I am gracious and constructively critical of salvation testimonies. I'm confident in the sender, the Spirit, but suspicious of how the messenger fiddled with the message before delivering it.

Though extremely rare, I cringe and mourn when I hear people say, "Sean changed my life." When I was a younger evangelist, in my immaturity, I secretly hoped that someone might say something like that; a comment like that would be the ultimate affirmation of my desire to make an impact in the life of another person ... or so I thought. Now, I confess how my younger aspirations are wrong and shallow. These desires subversively transformed my evangelistic message into "the good news of

whatever-I-can-say-to-get-a-response." More commonly, I hear newer Christians credit their church or parachurch ministry for their salvation. In my circles it is common for a teenager to say, "Young Life changed my life." For many years, the plain untruth and sadness of that statement didn't dawn on me. I'd like to say that my spiritual depth or theological expertise alerted me to the danger of crediting an organization with salvific power, but I wasn't aware for a long time of the dire implications. Crediting an organization or a person with salvific power is a version of breaking the first commandment. Organizations and people *will* fail you. It is not a matter of if but when. *When* this happens (and it will), the foundations of our faith often shaken.

When we commit to caring for souls, we are tempted to believe our care for others originates in us. No. We love (and care) because Christ first loved us (1 John 4:19). The origin of our pastoral care for others comes from the Shepherd of *our* souls. The only cornerstone worth building our proclamation of the good news upon is Jesus Christ. When Jesus Christ is the leading character in a salvation testimony, I have a sense that person is on firm ground, heading in the right direction, and the

messenger, the evangelist, thank God, acted with great wisdom when delivering the message.

The Message Matters Most

The key task of the evangelist is to deliver the message of the good news of Jesus Christ. While the noun "evangelism" only came into common use recently, that is not true about the word "evangelist." It is as ancient as the New Testament. How the church has spoken historically of the evangelist reveals the primacy of the content of the good news over techniques and methodologies that dominate modern discussions of evangelism. Like a newcomer to a white elephant gift exchange, people gravitate toward the largest box with the fanciest wrapping, only to find the contents of the box virtually empty. The New Testament evangelist, instead, is defined by the content of their message rather than external ribbons and bows intended to impress the recipient.

Paul told the Ephesian church that Christ provided evangelists alongside apostles, prophets, pastors, and teachers (Eph 4:11). We might expect Paul to explain that evangelists were meant to go out and share the gospel with nonbelievers.

Instead, Paul wrote that Christ created these roles collectively to "equip his people for works of service, so that the body of Christ may be built up" (Eph 4:12). The context of the passage introduces the term "evangelist" as a part of a team in a church that is "tossed back and forth by the waves, and blown here and there by every wind of teaching and by the cunning and craftiness of people in their deceitful scheming" (Eph 4:14). Paul addresses the content of what the church in Ephesus believes and teaches. Modern Christians need to be careful not to read back into this passage a picture of modern-day evangelists going door to door with tracts or holding outdoor rallies. While these tasks may be worthwhile evangelistic activities today, these were not the tasks of the evangelists Paul describes in the Ephesian church. The task of the evangelist in the Ephesian church concerns the *authentic content of the gospel* over and above other priorities.

Paul's words to Timothy, who was ministering in the Ephesian church, capture a similar evangelistic calling. Paul tells Timothy to "keep your head in all situations, endure hardship, do the work of an evangelist, discharge all the duties of your

ministry" (2 Tim 4:5). The phrases in this verse relate to each other and illuminate the task of evangelism. What was so difficult within the Ephesian church that Timothy must be told to "keep his head" and "endure hardship" as an evangelist? Is Paul telling Timothy to head out into the Ephesian neighborhoods and talk to strangers about Jesus? Is this the task that requires Timothy to practice restraint? No. Timothy's issue in Ephesus, paralleling the issue described in Ephesians 4:11–16, is that Timothy must confront people who will not "put up with sound doctrine." They, instead, "suit their own desires" and "gather around them a great number of teachers to say what their itching ears want to hear" (2 Tim 4:3). Paul, again, expects Timothy's evangelistic duties in the Ephesian church to center around authentic content and doctrine in the midst of what people erroneously *want* to hear. Biblical scholar Robert Yarbrough explains that Timothy's evangelistic duties are "the meat-and-potatoes of regular pastoral instruction and spiritual oversight. ... The core message of Christ's death and resurrection in accordance with the Scriptures must remain at the heart of all Timothy undertakes."[22]

Timothy's evangelistic duties focused on the pastoral work in Ephesus of announcing and reannouncing the authentic gospel amidst its alternatives. The pastor (the shepherd of souls) is forever evangelizing as he works in the realm of sanctification—reannouncing the gospel over and over again to converts and believers alike, as we will discuss further in chapter 6. The two passages explored above represent two of the three instances of the use of the word "evangelist" in the New Testament. The remaining instance is located in Acts 21:8 where Luke describes Philip, one of the seven appointed to serve the church (Acts 6:5) as an evangelist. Phillip went from distributing food to the poor in Acts 6 to being the first missionary to Samaria in Acts 8 because of the persecution in Jerusalem following Stephen's preaching and subsequent martyrdom.

Philip was among those who "preached the word wherever they went" (Acts 8:4). He "proclaimed the Messiah" and performed signs in Samaria (Acts 8:5–7). More specifically, we learn that Philip, "proclaimed the good news of the kingdom of God and the name of Jesus Christ" (Acts 8:12). People believed and were baptized

(Acts 8:12–13) because "Samaria had accepted the word of God" (Acts 8:14). Later, Philip shared the "good news about Jesus" (Acts 8:35) with the God-fearing Ethiopian eunuch before traveling and "preaching the gospel in all the towns until he reached Caesarea" (Acts 8:40).

God directed Philip's evangelistic travels in two interconnected ways: circumstances and the Spirit. Philip went to Samaria to flee the great persecution in Jerusalem. Yet, a closer look at the text shows that Luke describes Philip and the others as "scattered" in a passive sense, creating the question: Scattered by whom? Jesus prophesied the scattering of the gospel to Samaria as a work empowered by the Holy Spirit (Acts 1:8). Philip's encounter with the Ethiopian began by an angel telling him to go to the road from Jerusalem to Gaza before the Spirit told him to approach the Ethiopian's chariot (Acts 8:26, 29). Later, the Spirit redeployed the evangelist miraculously to another location (Acts 8:39). Modern evangelists can look to Philip's evangelistic ministry as an example of how evangelists must be attentive to how the Spirit of God works through circumstances.

Paul exhorted Timothy to do the work of an evangelist within the Ephesian church, and Luke

records how the Spirit prompted Philip to do the work of an evangelist in places that had not heard the gospel. Both evangelists had a common task: delivering the authentic content of the good news of Jesus Christ. Put in mathematical terminology: the variable is the context; the constant is the content. What this means is that evangelism can happen in many different situations. Evangelism can (and should) happen in a church, in an unevangelized country, on a road, or really anywhere. The context is not the defining characteristic of evangelism. The defining characteristic of evangelism is the message.

THE WORDS OF THE GOSPELS ARE THE GOSPEL

I remember the first time I attended a church service at Christ Church Anglican in Phoenix, Arizona. I was unfamiliar with the liturgical service. I was especially confused because two decades earlier the same church building had been the location of a wonderful charismatic non-denominational church I attended and served in for many years. Instead of reminiscing, I had to give my full attention to sitting, standing, and kneeling while following the lead of everyone around me. In a key moment of the service,

I forgot about those around me as I stood amazed (and yes, I was standing). After the other readings, the deacon walked into the midst of the congregation holding a gold-plated collection of the Gospels, lifted it up above his head, kissed it, and read the appointed Gospel reading.[23] While the tradition of reading the Gospels from the midst of the congregation only became popular among Episcopalians in the 1950s,[24] the special reverence for the reading of the Gospels goes back much further.

The substance of the message of evangelism was so strong in the early church that evangelists were not the people who delivered the message but the Gospel accounts (and their authors) themselves. Imagine for a moment that a modern-day evangelist arrived at a church, and when she walked through the door the crowd said, "Oh, fantastic, the evangelist is here!" She picks up her Bible and says, "Yes, the evangelists are right here!" In the early church if the Scriptures were on the pulpit and the pastor was at the back of the church and someone asked, "Where is the evangelist?" the congregation would turn their back to the pastor and point to the pulpit holding the Gospels. Why is this? This is because the early church understood that

the defining characteristic of evangelism was not the *messenger* but the *message* of the good news of Jesus Christ, shining most clearly in the four Gospel accounts of the Gospel writers.

The *Didascalia Apostolorum*, The Teaching of the Apostles, is a document from the early third century that gives us a snapshot of what early liturgical practice looked like. In it we read, "The Apostles have also decreed that at the end of all the Scriptures the Gospel shall be read as the seal of all the Scriptures, the people rising to their feet to hear it; because it is the Message of the Salvation of all men."[25] The Teaching of the Apostles was likely combined with other sources, such as the Didache, in the late fourth century to form the Apostolic Constitutions. The Apostolic Constitutions provides further details of the early liturgical service. This service consists of reading passages from the Old Testament, followed by readings from the book of Acts and the Epistles of Paul. After this, it explains, "While the Gospel is read, let all the presbyters and deacons, and all the people, stand up in great silence; for it is written: 'Be silent, and hear, O Israel.' (Deut. 27:9) And again: 'But do thou stand there, and hear.' (Deut. 5:31)."[26] What we see

is that the early church recognized a special place for the Gospels by standing in great silence during its reading. Further, the Gospels are described as "the Message of the Salvation of all men." The modern evangelist would be wise to follow this tradition and make the focal point of all evangelism the message of Jesus as presented in the four Gospels.

The early church understood the word "evangelist" as a noun describing the writers of the Gospels and the word "evangelical" as an adjective describing the content of the Gospels. The fourth-century bishop and church historian Eusebius provides a typical example of this usage; he wrote, "These things took place ... according to the statement of the holy Evangelists, who give the very words which [Christ] uttered."[27] Later, and in the same work, Eusebius illustrated the relationship between the Gospels, written by the evangelists, and the office of evangelists. He wrote, "Then starting out upon long journeys [the disciples] performed the office of evangelists, being filled with the desire to preach Christ to those who had not yet heard the word of faith, and to deliver to them the divine Gospels."[28] Eusebius understood the office of the evangelist as the delivery of the divine Gospels.

A century earlier, Origen made a similar distinction as he described the office of the evangelist as the narrator of the events of Jesus's life as an effort "intended to strengthen belief in the mission of Jesus."[29] The center of evangelism in the early church was the content of the four Gospels since the life, teaching, and ministry of Jesus are their explicit focal point.

I work in a ministry whose aim is to connect with the "furthest out" teenagers in our community. In our outreach meetings, our target audience is a young person with no familiarity with Christianity and who might never return to our meetings; we assume we only have one opportunity. But, if they show up, we *do* have one opportunity. When we have this one opportunity, I insist that when we open up our Bibles, we open to the Gospels. There are many pages we could turn to, and certainly the Holy Spirit can and does speak through all Scripture. Yet, I insist that the evangelists that I train and serve alongside preach out of Matthew, Mark, Luke, or John if our audience is truly people who really do not know the gospel. Evangelists must insist on the absolute center of our message, and I urge everyone to keep it simple: tell the story of Jesus over and over (and over). This is what the

early church did. In fact, they had a name for a summary of this story: the rule of faith.

The Rule of Faith

I have been married to Erin for over half of my life, and we dated for seven years before that, beginning as high-school sweethearts. I am an Erin expert. From time to time, I will meet someone new and be asked about Erin. I love when that happens, and I get excited to share about Erin because she is wonderful. But I'm faced with a dilemma: what do I say? I could say, "Buckle up, this story is going to take about a half a lifetime for me to share." If I want to share about Erin, I need to make some important decisions about summarizing what to say about her. When I do this, and no matter how well I do this, I'm going to leave out details of what I *could* say. My challenge becomes: what *must* I say about Erin? First, I must say things that are true. If I told you she is a huge fan of horror movies, I would be lying and describing someone else (she likes comedies). Second, I would be smart to say things that are essential to knowing Erin. For instance, it isn't essential to share her dislike for horror movies; it would be more important to tell you about her character: she is kind, gracious,

and always looking out for the overlooked. I might add a few basic details such as that she grew up in Phoenix, went to college in Spokane, Washington, teaches second grade, and is a mom of three teenagers. Within speaking a few sentences, I can provide a very basic summary of Erin. We do this all the time with people, ideas, and concepts. When I look up a topic that I don't know much about on Wikipedia, the first paragraph provides a quick summary of the details in the rest of the article. The rule of faith does this for what we *must* say about Jesus.

I want to address people like me that feel uneasy about summarizing. No matter what I say about Jesus, I am sad to know that my words are always incomplete. My evangelistic preaching always feels insufficient no matter what I say. Caring for souls feels like an unfinished task. I simply can't find sufficient words to capture what I'd want to say, neither in quality nor quantity. Thus, evangelists are likely to feel uneasy and incomplete in their delivery. I know that this is a simple function of the limits of being human, but it is important for evangelists to recognize the unsettling experience of the oversized task we are assigned to do. Not only is it important to recognize our inherent insufficiency

but we need to embrace it. We embrace this not going too far in either direction: saying too much or saying too little. We have to say something, knowing that "something" feels insufficient for the task. While the message might feel insufficient since it is always a summary, it isn't.

What must evangelists say about Jesus? The answer lies somewhere between the totality of the entire Bible and the beautiful two-word summary *kyrios Iesous*, Jesus is Lord (1 Cor 12:3; Rom 10:9; see also Phil 2:11; Acts 10:36). We should keep an eye on both extremes and ask: how does the entire Bible speak into the fact that Jesus is Lord? To do this well requires a solid understanding of the entire Bible; there are no shortcuts. But we do not, and should not, do this work on our own. We do not start from scratch in determining how to summarize the gospel. We trust that the Holy Spirit has guided our brothers and sisters in Christ throughout the history of the church to find a happy medium between all the words of the Bible and two words of the Bible. The happy medium, the reliable summary of the gospel that the church landed on, is the rule of faith.

The rule of faith is a summary of the basic facts of the gospel established in the early church based

upon apostolic preaching and teaching found in the Scriptures. Of the many examples, two are especially helpful. One is from Scripture itself:

> For what I received I passed on to you as of first importance: that Christ died for our sins according to the Scriptures, that he was buried, that he was raised on the third day according to the Scriptures. (1 Cor 15:3–4)

The other is the Nicene Creed.

We believe in one God,
  the Father, the Almighty,
  maker of heaven and earth,
  of all that is, seen and unseen.

We believe in one Lord, Jesus Christ,
  the only Son of God,
  eternally begotten of the Father,
  God from God, Light from Light,
  true God from true God,
  begotten, not made,
  of one being with the Father;
  through him all things were made.
  For us and for our salvation
  he came down from heaven:
  was incarnate

of the Holy Spirit
and the Virgin Mary,
and became truly human.
For our sake he was crucified
under Pontius Pilate;
he suffered death and was buried.
On the third day he rose again
in accordance with the Scriptures;
he ascended into heaven
and is seated at the right hand of the Father.
He will come again in glory
to judge the living and the dead,
and his kingdom will have no end.

We believe in the Holy Spirit,
the Lord, the Giver of Life,
who proceeds from the Father
[and the Son],
who with the Father and the Son
is worshiped and glorified,
who has spoken through the prophets.
We believe in one holy catholic
and apostolic church.
We acknowledge one baptism
for the forgiveness of sins.
We look for the resurrection of the dead,
and the life of the world to come.
Amen.

Many prominent early church theologians and pastors witnessed by the rule of faith. They used slightly different phrasing but always with the same key points: God is Father, Son, and Holy Spirit; Jesus is the one who reveals this God to us; this God creates, redeems, and sanctifies.[30] Tertullian wrote that to know the rule of faith is "to know all things."[31]

Jesus Is the Gospel

The core message is about God's acts in Jesus Christ. All evangelism must anchor its message in the person and works of Jesus Christ. The message of evangelism is Jesus Christ. Martin Luther wrote:

> The gospel, then, is nothing but the preaching about Christ, Son of God and of David, true God and man, who by his death and resurrection has overcome for us the sin, death, and hell of all men who believe in him. Thus the gospel can be either a brief or a lengthy message; one person can write of it briefly, another at length. He writes of it at length, who writes about many words and works of

Christ, as do the four evangelists. He
writes of it briefly, however, who does
not tell of Christ's works, but indicates
briefly how by his death and resurrection
he has overcome sin, death, and hell for
those who believe in him, as do St. Peter
and St. Paul.[32]

There is one essential ingredient, and it must be
the main ingredient, in every evangelistic message:
Jesus Christ. Yet, it can become incredibly tempting to substitute this ingredient for something
else in the pantry of options. Well-intentioned
Christians have accused my evangelistic ministry
of being shallow because we insist upon telling
the story of Jesus repeatedly. They imply that we
should move on to deeper topics, such as how to
develop a strong prayer life. When I hear this, I
smile in silence because I believe that if hearing
the gospel repeatedly is shallow, the shallowness is
with the hearer, not the message. I admit that as an
evangelist, and a theologian, I often want to move
other topics to the top, perhaps only mentioning
Jesus in passing from time to time. But when we do
this, we are not proclaiming an evangelistic message. We might be providing a useful and edifying

message, but not an evangelistic one; the good news isn't the good news without proclamation about Jesus.

The temptation to stray to other topics lures us into darker territory. When an evangelistic message focuses on human happiness and not Jesus, it is easy to spot the message is not about Christianity; it is a message of the world. The speaker is clearly talking about something else. If I described a short, extroverted woman who loves horror movies, those in the know would realize instantly that I'm not talking about my wife. This sort of gospel litmus test is not hard to acquire. The litmus test of the gospel, the rule of faith, is easy to ignore when alternatives tickle our ears and stomachs with great expediency. The gospel is always about death and life. The death of the Savior, the death of us, the resurrection of the Savior, and the new life and future resurrection of us. Promises of human happiness without our own death are evangelistic malpractice—worse than medical malpractice because the consequences are eternal.

The word of God promises both death and life for Christ and Christians. The basic contours of the rule of faith show us that Christ was incarnate,

born, died (crucified), and resurrected. Christians undergo something similar: birth, death, and resurrection. One of the many challenges of modern popular gospel proclamations is that they are not honest about the death that we must face in order to be born again. If we really believe that we can be born again *now*, then our life as we know it has to die *now*. If we believe that our baptism brings new life, we must also believe that by our baptism our old life was buried with him (Rom 6:4). Gerhard Forde asks, "How is it possible for God to get through to us at all?" and answers, "There is no cure; the patient must die."[33] Yet, the patient is not us; the patient was Christ. Our proclamation of the gospel must not dodge the prescription for the new birth: it requires death in order to bring life. But how does this happen?

We are saved and born again by faith in Jesus Christ. Faith is a gift. I want to repeat those four words again because upon them hinge heresy and hope: faith is a gift. Faith does not come from us. We can search our closets, garage, and all the rooms in our house for an item, wrap it up, put a bow on it, add a tag with our name on it, and open it in front of our friends, but that does not make it a gift; a gift, by definition, comes from

someone else. The most basic student of Scripture and theology knows that faith is a gift from God and not from ourselves (Eph 2:8). How does faith come to humans? Faith comes to humans through hearing the word of God. Reconsider the familiar words from Romans: "So faith comes from hearing, and hearing through the word of Christ" (10:17 ESV). God manifests faith in Christians through the word of Christ. The task of the evangelist is not to call, urge, beg, motivate, stir up, plead, implore, exhort, press, encourage, demand, solicit, pressure, request, or appeal for faith because faith is not a resource the hearer can supply. The task of the evangelist is to deliver the word of Christ. When evangelists deliver the word of Christ, our task is done. Sometimes the wind of the Spirit rustles leaves and we get to see and hear what is happening, but usually the work of the Spirit giving the gift of faith is invisible to us.

I do want to call, urge, beg, motivate, stir up, plead, implore, exhort, press, encourage, demand, solicit, pressure, request, and appeal to evangelists to do one thing: know your Bible. When you know your Bible, you begin to *speak* Bible. From time to time, I'll hear someone use a phrase and I'll think, "That sounds like something my grandma said."

When evangelists use the word of God, God brings conviction and (sometimes) life to lost souls who, often without knowing it, think, "That sounds like something my Creator said." The most powerful message evangelists can deliver, the message of first importance, is that "Christ died for our sins according to the Scriptures, that he was buried, that he was raised on the third day according to the Scriptures" (1 Cor 15:3–4). That is what the gospel sounds like.

CHAPTER 5

The Cadence of Announcing Jesus: Urgent Patience

But in your hearts revere Christ as Lord. Always
be prepared to give an answer to everyone who asks
you to give the reason for the hope that you have.
But do this with gentleness and respect.
—*1 Peter 3:15*

WHY IN THE WORLD WOULD YOU invite hundreds of friends and family to Phoenix, Arizona, in July, when temperatures can exceed 120 degrees? We had two reasons. First, churches and reception venues are cheaper and more available in the middle of the deadly heat of Phoenix summers (and rightly so). Second, I had recently graduated

college and we had waited long enough already. On July 8, 2000, Erin and I exchanged vows and celebrated the first day of our marriage. The day was a whirlwind of events, an intersection and reunion of our most important relationships and a defining moment for the promises we made to each other in our vows that established the nature of our marriage. Our marriage would not be the same without that important, exciting, and wonderful day. Our wedding day was essential to our marriage, but, in many ways, the story of our marriage began before July 8, 2000. Similarly, our marriage continues after our wedding day. The wedding day is essential to our marriage but to reduce our marriage to our wedding day would be to misunderstand what it means to be married.

WHEN A PARTY BECOMES A WEDDING

Since then, I have officiated many weddings. The day of a wedding is a whirlwind for everyone involved. Even among the most well-planned weddings scheduled with plenty of time for everything, the significance of the moment sweeps everyone up. It is a crazy day.

I've learned that many modern wedding ceremonies look quite different than what I remember

from my youth. Many modern wedding ceremonies don't follow tradition. You never know what might be next in the order of a wedding ceremony these days. So, when I meet with couples who have a bunch of wild ideas about what a wedding ceremony consists of, I stop them and make one thing very clear. I say, "I have some suggestions about what this wedding ceremony should include, but I only have one absolute requirement: you *must* make marriage vows to each other in the presence of God and those in attendance. Vows are required." Then, I often face another challenge; the couple frequently says they want to write their own vows. I reply, "That's wonderful, we can include those. But you are going to say traditional vows too." The vows in Christian marriage matter. They aren't up for customization. They can be worded differently, but they need to check several important boxes, and I make sure this happens.

The word of God—specifically the good news of the life, death, and resurrection of Jesus Christ—is essential to faithful authentic evangelism. When we care for souls in evangelism, our primary concern isn't to make someone feel cared for, it is to provide the care that God prescribes. Like wedding vows, the words of the gospel matter. If a

wedding lacked vows, I wouldn't consider it a wedding; I'd consider it a party. Parties happen all the time, and we all need a good party now and then. When you add vows to a party, it turns into a wedding. Evangelistic meetings and conversations are often more like parties and deeper-than-normal conversations, and we all need a good party and a good heartfelt conversation from time to time, but when you add the word of God, and those words are centered on Jesus Christ, you are evangelizing: the news you are sharing is the good news of Jesus Christ.

More Than One Chapter

While the word of God is the core of evangelism, we must keep the bigger picture in mind. Evangelism is not an isolated event. The rush of an evangelistic moment might climax in a first-time proclamation of faith, or a baptism, but to reduce evangelism to an isolated moment is to reduce a marriage to the vows of a wedding. An ongoing story precedes and proceeds the wedding day, which shapes the marriage along with the important and essential, but momentary, wedding ceremony.

Next to the door of our bedroom hangs a beautiful picture of Erin from our wedding day and a frame with our vows written in lovely calligraphy. Erin and I usually take time on our wedding anniversary to recollect, enjoy, and discuss our wedding vows. When Erin and I review our wedding vows, now several decades later, we see how the words we said that day have sprouted, grown, and matured in ways we couldn't have imagined earlier. We also recognize that the words we said on July 8, 2000, represent a snapshot in time of what was happening in our relationship on July 7, 2000, and all the days before. July 8, 2000, didn't happen spontaneously. It wasn't a party of strangers that just happened to end with vows. That day was part of a larger story.

Evangelists seeking to initiate people into the kingdom of God step into the story of people whose story is already in process. The message of the gospel stands outside of time. The *delivery* of the message comes through a person. When I was growing up, postal workers delivered mail to mailboxes in front of each house or to ones hung next to the front door. For many of us today, postal workers deliver our mail to a cluster mailbox in a

community area about a block away. Fortunately, the task of the delivery person is simplified and more efficient. Unfortunately, I don't know the name of the person who delivers my mail like I did when I was younger. Additionally, the comedic movie trope of a mail carrier entering a yard and evading the bite of an unfriendly dog or the splash of an unexpected sprinkler is no longer familiar. I have compared my work as an evangelist more recently with delivery folks because of the increase in various package and food delivery services.

I believe the gospel is best delivered personally and intimately. Cluster delivery might be efficient for mail but not for the gospel. There are many theological reasons for the embodied delivery of the gospel, but I want to share some pastoral wisdom regarding entering evangelistic relation-ships. Pastors who care for souls operate much like a physician who must first diagnose what is happening with the patient. Before you apply the proper treatment, you must provide a thorough diagnosis. Evangelism is a Spirit-led work; the Holy Spirit is the Lord and the giver of life. The primary metaphor and imagery in the Bible of the Spirit is the wind. I like to think of evangelistic pastoral diagnoses like gauging the wind. In any

given moment, I can stop, survey the movement of the leaves on the trees, lick my finger, and stick my arm toward the sky to become alert to what is happening right now. How should we do this? Before we get to the practical matters like praying, asking good questions, and listening well, I want to correct one of the biggest mistakes in evangelism: not understanding *our place and pace* in evangelism.

Calibrating Our Place and Pace

The current pace of the work of the Spirit in a person's life varies. A person might be standing in a hurricane or a gentle breeze. We see this variability in Scripture too. Most of the accounts in the Bible of people's lives are quite brief. Narrative accounts in the Bible generally capture a small window of time in a person's much longer life. When we look at the Gerasene demoniac in Mark 5, it looks like a spiritual hurricane, but there is a longer story that we don't have. Jesus's actions show us that what was required in that situation was a full-on sprint. Many of the evangelistic accounts in the Gospels and Acts are short and, at face-value, look more like spiritual hurricanes than gentle breezes. The vast majority of my evangelistic experiences, and

others I've observed, are rarely hurricanes, but I've seen a few.

For nearly a decade, I had an office inside of an older mainline church. One of the reasons that my office was in this church was because there were plenty of rooms available; the people and the church were dying. While it is not the case with all older mainline churches, the few people who came to the campus of this church were not familiar with the gospel. I knew this was true because I talked frequently to people who stopped by the church office. They would say to me, "What do you do here? You don't go to church here. Why do you have an office here?" I would tell them about my evangelistic work with young people, and they would normally reply with a kind but dismissive comment like, "Well, that's nice." Mary, the elderly secretary, was the absolute hub of the church. Mary was a vibrant Christian and organizational wonder woman who attended a different church but felt led by God to be the Monday-through-Friday secretary at this church. They needed Mary's talents because the church was busier with community programs and renting out meeting rooms on weekdays then on Sunday mornings. Mary was gifted

in many ways, but she was a bit shy in ministry situations.

One ho-hum Tuesday morning, I was making a flyer for an event when Mary rushed into my office and yelled, "Sean, can you run over to Room 127? I just called 911. An older man is dying, and I want you to pray for him." When I arrived, a man named Jim was on the ground and the paramedics had not yet arrived. Jim was alert but fading. I asked him if I could hold his hand. He said yes. I asked him if I could pray for him. Again he said yes. In the midst of my prayers for his health and comfort I asked, "Jim, have you ever responded in faith to Jesus, to trust him as Lord, the one who died for your sins?" Jim shook his head back and forth to signal no. I said, "Jim, today might be your final moment. Do you believe that Jesus is the Lord who died for your sins, and that he wants to welcome you into his kingdom?" Jim was losing his strength but nodded his head up and down. In a muted voice Jim said yes. Shortly thereafter, the paramedics rushed in. I stepped out of the way, and they attended to Jim and rushed him to the hospital. About an hour later, not knowing what to do, I returned to my office and finished making

the flyer I was working on earlier. The next day, I asked Mary how Jim was doing. She said that he survived, and his family was arranging for him to be moved across the state for long-term medical care. I never saw Jim again. I don't know what happened to him. That moment was a spiritual hurricane. I did my best to act quickly and faithfully. In that moment, I did the best I could. I am an imperfect messenger, not a savior.

Monsoon Season

In Phoenix, we have a wild and strange season called monsoon season. This season breaks up the other season we have in Phoenix, which we call "sunny and hot" (Phoenix averages three hundred sunny days per year). During monsoon season, which occurs between June 15th and September 30th, moisture surges north from the Pacific Ocean and Gulf of Mexico. When this arrives, the higher humidity combined with Phoenix's sizzling summer heat creates the perfect conditions for powerful desert storms. The storms bring drenching rain (sometimes as much as half the annual rainfall), blinding dust, damaging winds, and picturesque lightning. The intensity

of monsoon season varies considerably. If you have lived in Phoenix for a while, you always prepare for it each summer but never know what truly awaits you; sometimes several years will go by without any unusual activity. You just never know when the wind will pick up. However, when it does, you can bet that the local news will open every newscast, and flood their social media accounts, with breaking news and weather tracker updates.

Sam's parents pulled me into his storm. I received an unexpected phone call on a warm September afternoon from a concerned parent. His mom told me that her son Sam had just been expelled from a local Christian high school for selling drugs. Sam was a mess. The drugs were just the tip of the iceberg. His mom asked me if I could meet with Sam. I agreed. After an awkward first meeting, Sam and I decided to meet again and realized that we enjoyed spending time together. His parents continued to communicate with the school about Sam's progress. The school decided to readmit Sam if I would meet weekly to mentor him for a year. Somewhere in that year, Sam recalibrated his life and faith to be on a path that continues to this day, decades later.

The initial phone call I received felt a bit like breaking news in flashing letters, and for the first few weeks it felt like each day brought new details we could have labeled "Sam's weather tracker." Fortunately, the Sam news cycle slowed down, the dust began to settle, we cleaned up the broken branches strewn all over his life, and we began to slowly put things back in order through God's power and grace.

My entrance into Sam's life began with a bang, with a phone call of a few minutes. As the story continued, it transitioned to a meeting, then a year of meetings, and then a few decades of perspective. Sam's story began before I entered it, and it continued after the year or so that I spent with him. Sam's parents raised him as a Christian. Sam never knew himself otherwise and never rejected Christianity. In all honesty, I don't know if he has a conversion moment, and even as an evangelical and a vocational evangelist, I'm not concerned with figuring out when he was born again. Sam proclaims Jesus as his Lord, and his life bears the fruit of the Spirit. That's good enough for me.

When I was younger, I would sneak into the local movie theater and stay all day. Movie

previews show all the most exciting parts: the explosions, the passionate kiss, the hero hanging from a rope swinging below a flying helicopter. Movie previews are limited to about a minute, so they show the most dramatic scenes; they never show the long dialogues that provide the backstory. I came to realize many subpar movies share a common feature: they lack a backstory, and there is nothing more than climaxes. When a story is nothing but constant action, we naturally have a sense that there must be more to the story. The same is true with every person and, indeed, every Christian. Conversion testimonies rarely can be reduced to a sixty-second highlight.

The cadence of evangelism is slower than popular accounts of evangelism portray. William Abraham writes, "Most 'up-front' methods of evangelization assume that the person will make a sudden decision to follow Christ. ... The fact is that most people come to God much more gradually."[34] He is right. I am a vocational evangelist with over twenty years of experience, and I do not have a collection of many overnight conversion stories. Sometimes people tell their stories in "overnight" ways, but almost all my evangelistic

memories are long-term stories that I can see how they played out over time. I believe evangelists must commit to a slower and more patient cadence.

ATTEMPTING TO ACCELERATE EVANGELISM

On a cold Saturday afternoon, February 17, 1739, George Whitefield and his friend William Seward went to the coal-mining district, the colliers, of Kingswood, England. Outsiders seldom entered this rough and sometimes violent community, which lacked a school or church for the miners or their families. After gathering about two hundred people, Whitefield stood upon Hannam Mount, on Rose Green, and preached outdoors for his first time. Whitefield chose John 3:3 as his text: "Jesus answered and said unto him, Verily, verily, I say unto thee, Except a man be born again, he cannot see the kingdom of God" (KJV). Whitefield returned the following Wednesday and preached to two thousand people; two days later, he preached to over four thousand, and on Sunday an estimated ten thousand came to hear him preach. Whitefield's first open-air sermon is instrumental to understanding why I recommend

evangelistic patience today; in short, things are different now.

Whitefield and other early evangelicals believed that the people of England needed a bold and blunt awakening and challenge. Whitefield, Wesley, and others experienced the new birth and felt called by God to urge their hearers to experience it too. In 1737, Whitefield published a sermon that he believed began the awakening in England.[35] In this sermon, he challenged his hearers and asked them if they were Christians. He asked if they had a mere "outward profession of faith," or if they had "the inward reality of the baptism of the heart, in the Spirit." He asked if they had "experienced the glorious change of the soul." He said that Christ's redemption would not be complete unless the Spirit of God changed their natures. Whitefield challenged his hearers to be born again. To modern Christians, especially evangelicals, this might seem like a traditional evangelistic sermon, but to assume that would be a mistake.

In Whitefield's era, it is safe to assume that virtually all English speakers were Christians, at least in name and identification. It's estimated that 99.9 percent of people living in England and Wales between 1720 and 1760 were members of a

Christian congregation.[36] What this means is that the audiences of early evangelicalism are much different from modern audiences (more on that in a moment). Though early evangelicals had an urgent evangelistic message to share with Christianized audiences, they did not think they could accelerate the speed with which a person came to faith.[37] Some later evangelicals felt they could accelerate evangelistic success if the proper steps were taken; one such man was Charles Finney.

Charles Finney, sometimes called the father of modern revivalism, ministered in the early and mid-nineteenth century. He described conversion and regeneration in synonymous ways. Finney augmented the evangelical understanding of regeneration and thought it possible to ascribe regeneration to human initiative. At other times, he described conversion and regeneration as a product of simultaneous human and divine interaction. Finney believed that a minister could control the conversion and regeneration of a person. For him this process was scientific. He argued that revival "is a result we can logically expect from the right use of God-given means, as much as any other effect produced by applying tools and means."[38] He

added, "There is a long-held belief that the task of furthering Christianity is not governed by ordinary rules of cause and effect. ... No doctrine endangers the church more than this, and nothing is more absurd."[39] To accomplish this cause-and-effect process of revival and conversion, Finney advocated for three "new measures": anxious meetings, extended meetings, and the anxious seat.[40]

An anxious meeting is a meeting in which the minister spends personal prayer time with people in the meeting, often walking around the meeting from person to person. An extended meeting is a series of ongoing meetings that meet for multiple days or weeks in a row, like a multiday conference. Finney provided many practical tips for how to plan the meetings; these insights were marketing and logistical strategies. The anxious seat, introduced in 1830, was his most infamous "new measure." It could minimally be called an altar call, kneeling or raising a hand to indicate that you wanted to receive salvation, but it took its full form in a bench placed in the center of the congregation next to the pulpit in full view of everyone present. People went to the bench and sat on it when they were ready to receive salvation. Finney responded

to those who were critical of his promotion of the anxious seat tactic by arguing, "The apostles preached the Gospel to the people, and then all willing to be on Christ's side were called to be baptized. It held the same place the anxious seat does now: a public manifestation of determination to be a Christian."[41] For Finney, the anxious seat became a replacement for baptism, and it was quicker too. Finney boasted his preference for quick conversions: "Some of the best Christians I know were convicted and converted in a few minutes."[42]

Finney was not without his critics, but his success and his innovations influenced the practice of evangelicals significantly. Dwight Lyman (D. L.) Moody (1837–1899) built upon Finney's methods as he diligently advertised his campaigns, introduced an "inquirers room" where listeners could further inquire about salvation and make an instant decision to receive salvation,[43] and developed "decision cards" to capture the names and details of respondents (as well as provide details for local pastors to follow up). At the turn of the twentieth century, revivalists further embraced an evangelistic methodology that presumed a rapid evangelistic process and experience. Books and manuals on presenting the plan of salvation,

instructions about how to "pray Jesus into your heart," standardized "sinners' prayers," and evangelistic tracts including written prayers to receive salvation emerged with increasing frequency.[44] The legacy of Finney lives on within modern evangelicalism, with evangelicals rarely questioning the theology that lies behind evangelical methodology.

THREE MISTAKES OF
MODERN EVANGELISM

The history of evangelical theology and methodology forms modern-day assumptions about evangelistic practice. One key influence of this rarely examined heritage is the modern notion that the cadence of evangelism and the speed with which people come to faith happens quickly. This is a bad assumption to make. First, it is wrong to claim control of the speed of the movement of the Holy Spirit. Second, church history shows us that rapid conversions are not the norm. Third, modern studies of how people come to Christian faith, at least in America, tell a different story.

A study released in 2018 examined 1,788 people in America "who had made a new faith commitment or recommitment in the past year or so."[45] These commitments took the form of public

professions, baptisms, membership, confirmation, and other expressions.[46] The study found that 65 percent of evangelicals and 79 percent of nonevangelicals described their process as gradual and not something they could "put a date on."[47] The lead researcher of this study, Bryan P. Stone, concluded, "Even those who are first-timers to a faith tradition are likely to take one to three years. For a significant number, the journey is even longer than that."[48] An earlier study in the United Kingdom discovered that people described the process of coming to faith as a four-year journey.[49] The study also revealed "only 1 percent of Christians cite evangelistic events as the primary factor in coming to faith."[50] What this means is that effective modern evangelism is a slow process that is not built around events. Stone provides the following advice for evangelists: "For all the importance of other forms of outreach (literature, media, events, campaigns, and activities), it is still human relationships that are the number one factor for persons finding faith."[51] Conversion and regeneration, contra Finney, are a supernatural work of the Holy Spirit that cannot be controlled. At the same time, it appears that the trail of evidence that the Spirit leaves behind should instruct evangelists to

be patient in their work. Practically speaking, this means that wise evangelists will be patient with people as they become curious about genuine Christianity and are exposed to the word of God.

Another reason why modern evangelists should be patient in their approach is that the norms that many of us received from evangelicalism emerged from a culture which was Christianized in a much different way than our modern era. As mentioned above, when early evangelicalism emerged, 99.9 percent of people in England and Wales were part of a Christian church. The culture and nature of this engagement, with all its weaknesses, was much more extensive than the nominal Christianity observed in many modern Americans who identify as Christians. Americans are rapidly becoming less religious. In 1972, just one in twenty Americans said they had no religion; in 2018, that number was nearly one in four.[52] Sociologist Ryan Burge says one reason this has come about is because the internet has allowed people to communicate and find community for their views. Burge provides a helpful example: "A Mississippi atheist born in 1990 rather than 1960 would be more likely to find compatriots in the digital realm."[53] Today, there is less peer pressure to conform to community

religious norms because alternative communities are now easier to find than ever before. What is likely happening is not a decline in religiosity, but the emergence of true colors regarding religious identity. Burge writes, "Americans used to be Christians simply by default, not because of their belief in the words of the Apostles' Creed. Secularization merely gave permission for a lot of people to express who they truly are—religiously unaffiliated."[54] Unlike the days of Whitefield, Wesley, and Edwards, there is a massive lack of familiarity and experience with Christianity. Those earlier evangelists may have been able to call for conversion quickly, but modern evangelism has much groundwork to do relationally and in terms of educating people on the foundations of Christianity. All of this takes time and patience.

All three of my children, my son and two daughters, joined a fantastic sport which none of us understood: rugby. We began serving in a ministry with our friend Wil. We learned that Wil was the captain of the Arizona State University rugby team (we should have known from his massive physique, but that shows how unfamiliar we were with the sport). We went to a few of Wil's rugby matches, and my kids decided to give it a try (pun

intended). We joined a fun and supportive club in our local community. The coaches had all played rugby for decades and generously volunteered their time to help the kids. It was great. However, at times it became apparent that our coach James was stronger on personal experience than coaching ability. When games reached halftime, and when James was stressed, like most coaches at halftime, he would constantly implore the kids to "just … play … rugby!" Short on coaching wisdom and strong on gusto, James repeated louder and louder, "Just play rugby! Just play rugby!" He gave no further details except a long serious stare at each of the kids. The problem was no one on the team really knew how to play rugby. The kids had the uniforms, they knew the name of the team, and they were excited to be there, but they didn't know rugby—at least, they didn't know rugby like James knows rugby.

Modern evangelists face a similar challenge. We should not assume that our hearers know what we are talking about. Many Americans blend into the "team" of American Christianity but do not know Christianity. Motivational talks, gusto, and long stares are not needed. Given our current cultural milieu, Stone recommends, "For faith communities

interested in ministries of invitation, outreach, and inclusion, that means emphasis should be placed on accompaniment, formation, and education rather than solely tactics to get people in the door."[55] Again, all of this takes time and a patient cadence of evangelism.

Urgency through Patience

I have stressed the importance of a patient approach to evangelism. Someone might wonder if a patient approach contradicts the urgency of evangelism. It is easy to confuse urgency with importance. I believe a commitment to a patient approach to evangelism shows the urgency and importance of the task.

Jesus believed that his followers needed to carefully consider the cost of being a disciple; it wasn't something to rush into. Jesus likened becoming a follower to building a tower. A follower should "sit down and estimate the cost," because "if you lay the foundation and are not able to finish it, everyone who sees it will ridicule you, saying 'This person began to build and wasn't able to finish' " (Luke 14:28–30). Many evangelists sadly leave a trail of unfinished evangelism because of their foolish pace. Jesus's demands are not small. He

said, "Those of you who do not give up everything you have cannot be my disciples" (Luke 14:33). Giving up everything requires that you are thorough. Being thorough takes time.

The current and eternal misery of my friends and family who do not know the Lord Jesus Christ breaks my heart. The importance of this tragic situation couldn't be greater and is the reason why we must respond with great wisdom, which, as I have shown, requires great patience. First responders illustrate this well. Have you ever wondered why you rarely see paramedics and firefighters running to the scene of an emergency? This is because their instructors and supervisors taught them that it is more important to stay focused, safe, and assess the scene than to rush into it. When we rush, we fail to factor in the crucial details of our required tasks. I want to share a few tasks that are so important for evangelism and require great patience.

The first task is to foster a sense of belonging before demanding that a person believes in Jesus as Lord. Sometimes this approach is summarized as "belonging before believing." The ultimate location people need to feel like they belong is in your local congregation. Don't get me wrong,

the church service or liturgy will likely make them feel like they do not belong. Yet, if a nonbeliever knows people within the local church, they begin to feel like they belong. We must return the task of evangelism to the community of the local church. William Abraham writes,

> Since the middle of the nineteenth century evangelism has, for the most part, been cut loose from local Christian communities. Given the quest for autonomy, given the cult of individualism that is everywhere around us, given the drastic changes in communication, and given the deep antipathy there is to community and tradition, it is well-nigh impossible to link evangelism in an organic way with life in the body of Christ. To continue to construe evangelism as verbal proclamation is to ignore the radically changed sociological and ecclesiastical situation in which we have to work and to cling to the wrong kind of verbal continuity with the past.[56]

This is not to say that evangelism shouldn't happen outside of the brick-and-mortar church. It will.

But evangelists must see their task as a missionary function of their local church. The best way to help a nonbeliever feel like they belong in the kingdom of God is to build relationships with people inside the church. In a day and age when the most dynamic sermons and worship songs exist online and not at your church, the necessity for personal connection and belonging are more important than ever. How do you do this? You do this by patiently building relationships with people outside the church and help them meet people from the church. Do you send endless unrequested church event invitations to unbelievers to do this? No. The proper way requires much more patience: you must listen.

The second task requires urgent listening amid our urge to speak (or send invitations to events). Do you know why most people don't listen? It is because they are preparing to speak. I know people who spend hundreds of dollars per month so that someone will simply listen to them—that someone is their counselor. Counselors know what questions to ask, how to listen, and how to ask the right next question based on what they heard. If you were to look at the ratio of listening

to speaking, you would see that good counselors listen much more than they talk; the same is true of good evangelists.

Another place we must listen is in prayer. I don't claim to hear from the Lord in any unusual ways, but I know that when I pray for my friends who do not know Jesus, occasionally something happens. I sometimes have a sense of what to do or say next in my outreach with those people. Patient prayer for others is a way of listening to the Lord.

Rather than urging people to make a rash decision, the third task is to commit to informing, educating, and introducing people to the fullness of what it means to be a Christian. The Alpha course was developed in England in 1977 and over thirty million people worldwide have participated in it. The church Holy Trinity Brompton designed the class for people who have questions about faith in Jesus Christ, and it is widely deployed by churches as an evangelistic tool. Yet, Mark Ireland and Mike Booker write that the Alpha course "was originally designed as a discipleship tool for new Christians, but leaders quickly found that it was proving effective in reaching those who were not yet Christians."[57] Similar to "belonging before believing," the most effective order of evangelism might seem backward,

as in this task. Someone might ask, "Shouldn't a discipleship class come *after* a profession of faith?" Evangelism is strengthened by introducing a form of discipleship, education, and formation prior to a formal commitment to following Christ. None of these tasks eliminates the necessity of responding to the word of God; instead, these activities provide the opportunity for a person to "sit down and estimate the cost" (Luke 14:28) of following Jesus. A similar process of catechesis prior to baptism is common in church history but largely forgotten by many churches today.[58] This is unfortunate since 96–98 percent of people who participated in an instructional class prior to coming to faith found it helpful.[59]

A final task is the courage to ask friends what they think of Jesus Christ. This task might seem blunt, and it might be from time to time, but it requires patience. If someone responds positively, you need evangelistic wisdom about the next best step for them. If someone responds negatively (or even more disheartening, neutrally), patience is required to not read too much into it or overreact. If this task is taken in isolation from the other tasks (such as approaching a stranger to talk to them about the gospel), this task will likely be

difficult. But if this conversation fits within the other activities we've explored, it is much more natural. Patience in these conversations is needed because people rarely come to faith the first time they hear the gospel. Instead, the word of God is meant to be announced and reannounced.

CHAPTER 6

Reannouncing Jesus

*Now, brothers and sisters, I want to remind you of
the gospel I preached to you, which you received and
on which you have taken your stand.*
—*1 Corinthians 15:1*

I WAS ON A SPIRITUAL HIGH THAT AFTERNOON
in Oregon. At least, that was what my friends
called it back in the '90s. It was as if I had spiritual caffeine running through my body—every bit
of me was excited, eager, and energetic about my
faith in Christ. I look back now and realize that,
while I admire the enthusiasm of my younger years,
I had a lot to learn.

When I was nineteen years old, I was chosen
to serve on a month-long service team at a resort
camp on the coast of British Columbia, Canada.
It was a dream come true. The location of this

property still leaves my jaw on the ground. Located on an inlet of the Pacific Ocean, it is only accessible by a several-hour boat ride or by seaplane. The camp is nestled between mountains capped with glaciers that extend toward the sky, which create waterfalls on a bay where orcas swim in the summer. It is stunning in every sense of the word. Not only did I get to be there for a month, but I was chosen to be on the leadership team. To top it all off, I received a free trip to Seattle two months before our event to gather for training. That is how I ended up stopping for an afternoon in Oregon.

The trip to Seattle for training was my first step into vocational Christian ministry. It was a big step for me, and I knew it. I knew it because the organization paid for my airline ticket to Seattle (and the rest of the trip too). An airline ticket was a big deal to me because I rarely went on vacations as a young person and even fewer flights—and now, I was getting all of this for free. Three years prior, I knew nothing about Jesus Christ. I was there, in that moment, thinking, "Here I am!" gleaming with excitement and pride about the trajectory of my life and faith. My flight from Phoenix to Seattle had a three-hour layover in Portland. As someone who had rarely been on a vacation, much less an

airplane, I decided to make the most of my layover. Despite the tight window of time, I exited
the plane in Portland, rushed out of the airport,
jumped on a city bus, and took the twenty-minute
ride to explore downtown Portland. I only had fif-
teen minutes in downtown Portland before I knew
I needed to find a bus back to the airport. Those
minutes were magical, like a movie when a little
girl looks up at the sky and spins around in a big
sparkly dress for the first time as the camera looking down at her zooms up higher and higher. I
was lost in the moment. For me, it was a spiritual
moment; I was on a spiritual high. That is when
I decided to "share the good news" with anyone
I could in downtown Portland while I had the
chance.

Despite my enthusiasm, I wasn't sure who to
tell the good news, and I was equally unsure of
exactly what I would say. I remember standing in a
park near some young people embodying the complete package of the grunge era: unkempt hair, gui-
tars strewn about, torn clothes, and "I don't care"
attitudes souring their faces. I wondered how to
approach them. I was intimidated and confused.
"This must not be the Lord's will for them today," I
thought to myself and decided to move on. With

time running out, I decided to be bolder in my very itinerant evangelistic crusade. As I stood at the bus stop waiting for my bus back to the airport, I noticed another bus was about to depart. With my heart racing with nervousness and my "spiritual high," I ran inside the bus, looked a Portlandia-esque woman in her face, and proclaimed to her, "Jesus loves you and died for you!" Seconds later, I saw the bus doors starting to close behind me, so I darted back out, entered my bus heading back to PDX, and gleamed with pride having done the hard work of an evangelist for the lost people of Portland.

I look back at that experience with spiritual nostalgia and embarrassment. I know there is a very remote chance the woman I encountered that day needed to hear those seven words; but, in all honesty, the moment was entirely about me and what was happening in my life that day. For a moment, let's think through the experience of that woman and ask: were those words enough?

WHICH GOSPEL IS ENOUGH?

When we share the good news, it is always partial. The sermons in the book of Acts vary in length, so do the various statements of the rule of faith in

the early church. At minimum, the announcement of the good news might be as brief as "Jesus is Lord." This announcement could grow to include every page of the Bible from beginning to end. Perhaps this message could stretch to include Martyn Lloyd-Jones's seven-thousand page, four-teen-volume exposition of the thirteen-page epistle to the Romans written by Paul who announced simply: "The good news is about his Son" (Rom 1:3). Which version of the announcement of the gospel is "enough" to qualify as the good news?

God's word is special because the Spirit of God is in God's words. The exact number and arrangement of God's word, and the gospel, can vary, because the Holy Spirit makes those words meaningful and affective. God spoke through Paul to write, "Therefore I want you to know that no one who is speaking by the Spirit of God says, 'Jesus be cursed,' and no one can say, 'Jesus is Lord,' except by the Holy Spirit" (1 Cor 12:3). When anyone at any time says the words "Jesus is Lord," those words are meaningful. An intersection exists where meaningful words meet open ears. Recall the Lord's words to Isaiah, spoken also by Jesus in his parable of the soils: "You will be ever hearing but never understanding; you will

be ever seeing but never perceiving" (Matt 13:14). The Spirit chooses to use the meaningful words of God's word in different ways. Martin Luther taught that only the Spirit of God truly teaches the word of God:

> No one can correctly understand God or His Word unless he has received such understanding immediately from the Holy Spirit. But no one can receive it from the Holy Spirit without experiencing, proving, and feeling it. In such experience the Holy Spirit instructs us as in His own school, outside of which nothing is learned but empty words and prattle.[60]

The meaningful words of the gospel can fall on deaf ears or eager ears because, as Luther says, the Holy Spirit controls their effectiveness.

The work of God arrives in human lives through the Holy Spirit, yet the normal operation of the Holy Spirit comes through humans speaking God's word, and thus, the gospel. Paul writes, "So faith comes from hearing, and hearing through the word of Christ" (Rom 10:17 ESV). If you want to

see the Holy Spirit work in your ministry, speak God's words to people. Luther, again, has something to teach us on this point. Luther writes, "It's decreed that the external word must be preached and come first. Once we have the word enter our ears and we grasp it with our heart, the Holy Spirit—the true schoolmaster—comes and gives the word power, so that it takes root. ... And so we must honor the gospel and grant it this praise: that it is a means and way—just like a pipe—through which the Holy Spirit flows into and enters our hearts."[61] We preach the external word, the external gospel, anchored in the rule of faith, and after that, we let go because we do not know what will happen next. The Holy Spirit who "gives power to the Word" sets the internal work of God loose. The words emerging from the lips of the evangelist, the external words, are just words; when the words are met by the Spirit a conduit forms through which words become the Word.

WORDS FROM A CLOWN

My friend Steve and his sister Amy didn't grow up in a Christian home. When Steve was in high school, he heard the gospel and the Spirit of God

worked in his life to bring him to faith in Christ. Soon thereafter, Steve wanted his sister to know Jesus, so he told her the gospel. Amy wasn't interested. Steve was sad and confused. He asked himself, "How could Amy not want to respond to the best news I have ever heard?" The following week, Steve reannounced the good news to Amy. She politely declined. Steve was discouraged but didn't give up. He talked to a mentor, read a pamphlet with evangelistic tips, and tried again. Same response. This cycle repeated for weeks, months, and years. Steve attempted every combination of words and strategies he could find, but Amy simply wasn't interested.

Amy moved to a different state and her conversations with Steve became less frequent. Years later, Steve's phone rang, and when he answered he was happy to hear Amy's voice. Amy told him, "Steve, I have some great news to tell you. I am a Christian." Steve was thrilled and relieved. While he was caught up in the moment and sharing in her joy, he could not help thinking to himself, "Finally! The gospel I shared with her countless times made sense to her."

After celebrating with her for a few minutes, Steve asked Amy a question he was sure he knew

the answer to. He asked, "How did it happen?" He expected Amy to explain how his repeated evangelistic efforts finally made sense to her. Instead, and much to his dismay, she told him what happened. Amy said, "It was the craziest thing. I was watching a football game with some friends at a party. I don't normally pay attention to the game much, but I looked at the screen when the kicker kicked the extra point for the field goal, and there was a guy with a massive rainbow clown wig in the crowd holding a sign above his head with the words 'John 3:16.' I don't know what it was, but something about it made me curious. I found a Bible and read that Bible verse. In that moment I realized that I was a sinner and needed Jesus to save me." Steve wished he was more excited, instead he was frustrated. Steve thought to himself, "After all the years of conversations, prayers, and efforts ending in failure, a guy with a clown wig and a sign that never talked to Amy gets the job done?" Steve told me this story a decade after the clown sign incident; Amy's Christian faith is mature and genuine since that day. The Spirit of God controls the effectiveness of the word of God. Caring for souls through the task of evangelism is to announce the good news of Jesus Christ not just

once, but repeatedly because we never know how the Spirit might use God's word. The Holy Spirit controls the effectiveness of God's word.

ANNOUNCE AND REANNOUNCE

A simple reading of the New Testament, especially the Gospels, through a modern evangelical lens might leave the reader thinking that the way the gospel message works is like an ultimatum. For instance, when we read Jesus saying, "Come, follow me" to Peter and Andrew and then read, "At once they left their nets and followed him" (Matt 4:18–20), it gives the appearance that an immediate response is the paradigmatic and normative response to Jesus's call to follow him. A few chapters later, Jesus said to Matthew, "Follow me," and next we read, "Matthew got up and followed him" (Matt 9:9). After Peter's inaugural sermon in Acts, his listeners were "cut to the heart" and asked, "What shall we do?" Peter replied, "Repent and be baptized, every one of you, in the name of Jesus Christ for the forgiveness of your sins. And you will receive the gift of the Holy Spirit." Then Luke tells us that, "Those who accepted his message were baptized, and about three thousand were added to their number that day" (Acts 2:37–38, 41).

These well-known Bible accounts make evangelism look like a simple and rapid one-time event. A one-time approach to announcing the gospel can be read into Jesus's instructions to his disciples, whom he told, "If anyone will not welcome you or listen to your words, leave that home or town and shake the dust off your feet" (Matt 10:14). Reading these passages as evidence of one-and-done preaching of the gospel leads to beliefs such as evangelist T. L. Osborn's oft-repeated statement, "No one should hear the gospel twice until everyone has heard it once."[62] Put simply, this is wrong. The Bible rarely depicts a one-and-done announcement of the gospel, as we will see in just a moment.

Consider the experience of the apostle Peter. Peter initially responded to Jesus's call to "follow me." As we know, Peter told Jesus that he would never deny him (Matt 26:35; Mark 14:31). Yet, Peter denied his knowledge of Christ three times, as recorded in each of the four Gospels (Matt 26:69–75; Mark 14:66–72; Luke 22:55–60; John 18:16–27). Jesus appeared to Peter before appearing to the other apostles (Luke 24:34; 1 Cor 15:5). Later, Jesus reinstated Peter and concluded his conversation with Peter by reannouncing to Peter,

"Follow me" (John 21:19, 22), just as he did when he first called him. While we don't know the individual details of the other followers of Jesus, we do know that the apostle Thomas faltered in his belief. Thomas, the one who said, "Let us also go, that we may die with [Jesus]" (John 11:16) also said he would not believe that Jesus resurrected unless he touched Jesus's wounds (John 20:25). Thomas had become a nonbeliever in Jesus's promises. Similarly, at Jesus's Great Commission we learn that the eleven disciples saw Jesus, worshiped him, "but some doubted" (Matt 28:17). Some of the people who spent the most time in history with the incarnate Lord Jesus Christ in his life and resurrection still required further words from Jesus in order to continue their belief. Their experience was certainly not a one-and-done experience. The apostles needed to hear the good news more than once, and so should we.

It should not surprise us that Jesus's call and message, the good news of God, needs to be announced and reannounced, for this is what the Lord asked the Old Testament prophets to do. For instance, the Lord spoke through Jeremiah to tell the Israelites how they could stay alive in

the face of the Babylonians' attack (Jer 21:9), and then he repeats the same message in Jeremiah 38:2–3. Similarly, the prophets repeated a similar message to Israel that "to obey is better than sacrifice" (1 Sam 15:22; Isa 1:12–17; Prov 21:3).

Paul's custom was to return repeatedly to the local synagogues to preach that Jesus is the Son of God. For example, "Saul spent several days with the disciples in Damascus. At once he began to preach in the synagogues that Jesus is the Son of God" (Acts 9:19–20). Similarly, we read, "At Iconium Paul and Barnabas went as usual into the Jewish synagogue" (Acts 14:1). Again, Luke explains, "As was his custom, Paul went into the synagogue, and on three Sabbath days he reasoned with them from the Scriptures, explaining and proving that the Messiah had to suffer and rise from the dead" (Acts 17:2–3; see also 13:5, 17:10–11, 16–17; 18:1–11, 19–20; 19:8–10). Paul's repeated return, often to the same synagogue, is evidence of the need to announce and reannounce the good news of Jesus.

The sermons in Acts provide another example of the need to announce and reannounce the gospel. There are instances where the preaching of

the gospel in Acts, seemingly in the first instance, provokes an immediate response. We see an immediate response to Peter's Pentecost sermon when the people ask, "What shall we do?" Peter tells them to repent and be baptized, and they did (Acts 2:37–41). We observe something similar when Peter preaches to a group of people at Solomon's Colonnade in Acts 3; we learn that "many who heard the message believed" (Acts 4:4). Later, in Acts 10, Peter preaches and suddenly, "While Peter was still speaking these words, the Holy Spirit came on all who heard the message" (Acts 10:44).

In Acts we also observe instances where preaching does not illicit an immediate response, such as Peter's preaching in Acts 4:10–12. Several times in Acts we see the initial announcement and then the reannouncement of the good news of Jesus. For instance, in Peter's proclamation in Acts 5:30–32, there are no details about the response given, but we do learn that "day after day, in the temple courts and from house to house, [the apostles] never stopped teaching and proclaiming the good news that Jesus is the Messiah" (Acts 5:42). The apostles proclaimed the good news that Jesus is the Messiah in the temple courts and in homes

"day after day." The message was the same and it was repeated; it was reannounced. Paul and Barnabas's preaching in Acts 13:17–41 appears to result in no immediate response; instead, "the people invited them to speak further about these things on the next Sabbath" (Acts 13:42). The need for patience and reannouncement of the gospel might be most pronounced in Paul's proclamation to King Agrippa in Acts 26. Paul concludes his sermon by telling Agrippa, "I am saying nothing beyond what the prophets and Moses said would happen—that the Messiah would suffer and, as the first to rise from the dead ..." (Acts 26:22–23), mirroring the summary we discussed in chapter 4 regarding the core content of the gospel. Paul says that Agrippa is "familiar with these things," and asks, "King Agrippa, do you believe the prophets? I know you do" (Acts 26:26–27). Agrippa said to Paul, "Do you think that in such a short time you can persuade me to be a Christian?" (Acts 26:28). Thus, there are times that the proclamation of the gospel in the sermons in Acts brings an immediate response, but also the proclamation of the gospel often needed to be explained and re-explained, announced and reannounced, with great diligence and patience.

We must reannounce the gospel repeatedly to people who do not believe and to those who do believe. What do we do then with Paul's words to the church in Rome? He writes, "It has always been my ambition to preach the gospel where Christ was not known, so that I would not be building on someone else's foundation" (Rom 15:20). Does this verse demonstrate a paradigm for evangelists to employ a one-and-done presentation of the gospel? Not at all. The evidence from Paul's preaching in Acts explained earlier shows that his routine was to hunker down and stay in a community for weeks at a time, if not longer, reannouncing and re-explaining the gospel. Paul had a personal calling from Jesus to bring the gospel to the gentiles; Paul is not saying that his calling and ambition will be the same for all Christians. Paul wrote his letter to the church in Rome, which is a church that he didn't announce the gospel to. Yet Paul was happy to write to them and assist them, and he was eager to visit them in person. We can understand the entire letter to the Romans as the reannouncement of the gospel. Paul told the Corinthian church, "I want to remind you of the gospel I preached to

you" (1 Cor 15:1). Similarly, Paul did not hesitate to remind the Corinthians what he had already passed along to them regarding the Lord's Supper, which proclaims the Lord's death until he comes (1 Cor 11:23, 26).

Scripture provides clear examples and instructions to announce and reannounce the gospel. Recent studies show the importance of this task. A study in England in 1990 by Bishop John Finney found that it took, on average, four years for an adult to make a new faith commitment.[63] In 2013, Bryan P. Stone at Boston University School of Theology undertook a similar study on a larger scale in the United States. He found that only 35 percent of evangelicals, and 21 percent of none-vangelicals understood their adult conversion as sudden enough that they could "put a date on it."[64] The vast majority of people who came to faith as adults understood their conversion as much more gradual, with the median time across all Christian traditions being three years and the range being from a month to fifty years.[65] Evangelists, therefore, should always adopt a long-term and ongoing approach to announcing the gospel for both biblical and practical reasons.

FALSE DIVIDE

One reason many Christians lack a commitment to reannouncing the gospel is because they insert a false divide between evangelism and discipleship, seeing these as two separate and isolated tasks. It is common to hear someone say, "I was saved and then discipled." While this comment is frequently a simple and honest explanation of many Christians' understanding of their experience, it creates a shallow and unhelpful understanding of both evangelism and discipleship.

This book's goal isn't an in-depth discussion of discipleship, but discipleship requires a relationship; discipleship is not a task or a meeting. Discipleship involves knowing and interacting with a person. Because of this, we can be disciples of anyone. John the Baptist had disciples, so did the Pharisees because the core meaning of discipleship is to be an apprentice-learner through a relationship with a master. With that concept in place, we can see that discipleship begins frequently prior to conversion or hearing the gospel—as it did with John the Baptist's disciples and those of the Pharisees. What happens often in evangelism is that a genuine and trusting relationship is established in which the non-Christian sees something

in the Christian that makes the person curious. At this point, discipleship has already begun.

One of my neighbors is not a Christian, but I know that my neighbor is curious and a bit confused about why my family and I live the way we do. In this sense, I am already discipling my neighbor. In time, Lord willing, my neighbor will come to faith, and I hope to be a part of that process and walk with my neighbor in his next steps of faith. But at that time, I need to begin to step out of the way; my neighbor needs to become a disciple of Jesus, not a disciple of me. This is exactly what John the Baptist did when his disciples left him (John 1:35–37). Later, John's disciples commented that everyone was leaving him and going to Jesus; John replied, "The bride belongs to the bridegroom. The friend who attends the bridegroom waits and listens for him, and is full of joy when he hears the bridegroom's voice. That joy is mine, and it is now complete. He must become greater; I must become less" (John 3:29–30). Evangelists serve as friends of the bridegroom, and we wait joyfully for his voice to call his bride—and then we step out of the way.

The false divide between evangelism and discipleship persists because of a shallow transactional

view of evangelism. Evangelism is the announcement and reannouncement of Jesus Christ. When faith meets this announcement, a dead person comes alive. But alive for what? For heaven? Heaven forbid God brings us from death to life simply to send us to a better destination. No! God is not our divine vacation planner. God delivers us from death to life so that we can *know* God. And we are meant to know God *now*. Our salvation brings us eternal life, and Jesus defines eternal life for us: "Now this is eternal life: that they know you, the only true God, and Jesus Christ whom you have sent" (John 17:3). Eternal life is knowing God, and his Son, Jesus Christ. Evangelism, like discipleship, is all about knowing and relating to Jesus Christ.

God desires for all people to know him now—right *now*, not just at some later date in heaven. When we understand God's intention this way, we make better sense of the phrase "good news" and the word "gospel" in the Gospels that exist prior to the death and resurrection of Jesus Christ. For instance, how is it that Mark can tell us that at the beginning of Jesus's ministry, "Jesus went into Galilee, proclaiming the good news of God" (Mark

1:14)? What "good news" could Jesus be sharing with people prior to his death and resurrection? When we read further in the Gospels, we see that Jesus himself *is* the good news. Jesus proclaimed the good news of the kingdom of God because Jesus is the king of the kingdom. Jesus told the Pharisees who were looking right at him, "The kingdom of God is in your midst" (Luke 17:21). The goal of evangelism is a right relationship with God and his Son, Jesus Christ, so that we can become a participating member of God's eternal kingdom right now.

We must reannounce Jesus to non-Christians who need to hear the message until the Spirit gives the gift of faith. We must reannounce Jesus to Christians because we are always in need of refreshing and refocusing our relationship with God and others as we participate in God's kingdom work. My children know on their birthdays they will hear mom and dad tell stories about their births. On our wedding anniversary, my wife and I enjoy retelling the stories about our wedding day. So it is with reannouncing the gospel to Christians: we recount the stories we already know about how the groom calls his bride.

Gospel Depth and Maturity

The reannouncement of the gospel should surround the people of God everywhere we find ourselves. However, I frequently encounter people who divide evangelism and discipleship. These well-intentioned Christians look at the proclamation of the gospel like learning all the state capitals in elementary school—something everyone must do—but mature Christians need to move on to more important things. When people ask me what my ministry is teaching right now, and it almost always has something to do with the gospel, I commonly hear, "When are you going to move on to the 'deep stuff'?" When I hear this, my heart sinks within me. It's true that I'm offended by the accusation of having a shallow ministry. But my heart also breaks for the person standing in front of me because I believe the shallowness is their understanding and engagement with the gospel; they fail to see that the holistic task of caring for souls includes an initial and recurring announcement that Jesus is Lord.

When we reannounce the gospel to Christians, we are not starting over from square one. The author of the book of Hebrews warned against this

approach. The readers of Hebrews are to "move beyond the elementary teachings about Christ and be taken forward to maturity, not laying again the foundation" (Heb 6:1–2). The foundation includes repentance, faith, cleansing rites, laying on of hands, resurrection, and eternal judgment (Heb 6:2–3). It would be a grave mistake to assume that Christians shouldn't talk about these topics. Imagine a church that never talks about faith or their hope in the resurrection. These topics are, as stated in Hebrews, foundational. Ignoring foundational truths is not a sign of maturity, but immaturity. The author of Hebrews urges readers to "not lay again" the beginning of these topics. There is a difference between talking about faith and repentance with someone who has never considered them and reminding a Christian about the importance of faith and repentance. Charles Spurgeon wrote, "Let us go on believing and repenting, as we have done; but let us not have to begin believing and begin repenting."[66] From time to time, friends of ours invite us to celebrate their anniversaries by throwing a massive party to renew their wedding vows, but no one in attendance understands the event as the beginning of their marriage; neither

does anyone think the event is a sign of immaturity—quite the opposite, it is a sign of marital maturity.

What does reannouncing the gospel look like for mature Christians? Keep telling Christians about Jesus. The best place for this announcement is in the church. A frequent opportunity for the reannouncement of the gospel is at the end of the sermon. In some traditions, it is common to end a sermon by connecting the sermon to the gospel, to Jesus Christ. If the primary audience for this proclamation includes people who have never heard the gospel before, address them explicitly. Whether a sermon is ten, thirty, or sixty minutes long, all sermons can use an "I'm talking to you" moment at the end. Address nonbelievers with a specific challenge related to the gospel and address believers with their own challenge. While the substance of these challenges are the same—the challenge should proclaim Jesus's life, death, and resurrection for our sins—no one would mistake a wedding ceremony for a wedding-vow renewal ceremony. Another reason to be clear about your audience is that you do not want Christians to become "too familiar" with the facts of the gospel—as if the real sermon just ended and now is the part that

doesn't apply to me. The solution is: be clear. Say, "I want to speak to those of you who have not yet responded in faith," and then, "For those of you who have faith in Jesus Christ, receive this word again today."

Another time to reannounce the gospel in the church is in the sacraments of baptism and the Lord's Supper. Baptism is an obvious event for the proclamation of the beginning of faith; it is also a place for the reannouncement of the good news to the rest of the congregation. Martin Luther taught we are to daily renew our baptism.[67] We rise and say, "I am baptized into Christ." Consider the Book of Common Prayer's "Renewal of Baptismal Vows":

Bishop	Do you, here in the presence of God and the Church, renew the solemn promises and vows made at your Baptism and commit yourself to keep them?
People	I do.
Bishop	Do you renounce the devil and all the spiritual forces of wickedness that rebel against God?

People	I renounce them.
Bishop	Do you renounce the empty promises and deadly deceits of this world that corrupt and destroy the creatures of God?
People	I renounce them.
Bishop	Do you renounce the sinful desires of the flesh that draw you from the love of God?
People	I renounce them.
Bishop	Do you turn to Jesus Christ and confess him as your Lord and Savior?
People	I do.
Bishop	Do you joyfully receive the Christian Faith, as revealed in the Holy Scriptures of the Old and New Testaments?
People	I do.
Bishop	Will you obediently keep God's holy will and commandments, and walk in them all the days of your life?
People	I will, the Lord being my helper.[68]

These vows, recited by the baptized in the congregation, are vibrant and interactive reannouncements of the gospel.

The Lord's Supper is another natural opportunity to announce and reannounce the gospel to the church. Many churches rightly rehearse Paul's words from 1 Corinthians 11:23–26 when partaking of the meal. We should also remember Jesus's words from the night he was betrayed (1 Cor 11:23) in which we recall that Jesus told his disciples that the cup is "my blood of the covenant, which is poured out for many for the forgiveness of sins" (Matt 26:28). We also remember Jesus's challenging words to his disciples earlier in his ministry, "Very truly I tell you, unless you eat the flesh of the Son of Man and drink his blood, you have no life in you. Whoever eats my flesh and drinks my blood has eternal life, and I will raise them up at the last day" (John 6:53–54). The Lord's Supper, therefore, reannounces the forgiveness of sins and eternal life. Protestants can choose the language that fits their tradition, but all traditions have the opportunity in their celebration of the Lord's Supper to reannounce the gospel to Christians.

Another opportunity to reannounce the gospel with the gathered church is in the confession and absolution of sin. To be clear, many Protestants deny any salvific efficacy of absolution as if it comes from the pastor's own power and instead affirm absolution as the pastor's declaration of God's forgiving mercy. Some churches avoid public confession (and absolution), and instead choose various forms of corporate church discipline. Those who choose to celebrate public confession and absolution provide a powerful opportunity to reannounce the good news of the gospel. For example, consider the words of absolution provided in the Book of Common Prayer following confession:

> Almighty God, our heavenly Father, who in his great mercy has promised forgiveness of sins to all those who sincerely repent and with true faith turn to him, have mercy upon you, pardon and deliver you from all your sins, confirm and strengthen you in all goodness, and bring you to everlasting life; through Jesus Christ our Lord. Amen.[69]

Outside of the church, we can and should reannounce the gospel in our homes. Praying the Lord's Prayer provides us an opportunity to address God as "Our Father," which is a profession of faith; it focuses our attention on God's kingdom, the repeated focal point of Jesus's good news of the kingdom of God; and it draws our attention for our need of forgiveness for our sins (our trespasses). Even when we pray this prayer alone, we are never alone because the prayer is a plural prayer, "*Our* Father." It is the prayer of Jesus and the entire church.

I live in a desert, literally. You could walk out my front door and within one minute step into the Sonoran Desert. The Sonoran Desert stretches over 100,000 square miles of Arizona, California, and northern Mexico. This climate is arid and incredibly hot. Phoenix receives 9 inches of rain in 33 rainy days per year while the average in the United States is 38 inches of rain over 106 days. Most of the rainy days in Phoenix are during the intense monsoon season in summer. For the rest of the year, it is bone dry. When I see raindrops, I feel like celebrating in the streets. It is a salve for the dry ground of our city and our home. Announcing

and reannouncing Jesus is the salve and refreshing rain our souls long for. The proper response to hearing the good news of God is for our souls to want to dance in the streets. There are many words we can use in our ministries, but I beg you to provide the refreshment our dry souls long for by reannouncing the good news of Jesus again and again. Our hearts cry out with the psalmist, "My soul faints with longing for your salvation, but I have put my hope in your word. My eyes fail, looking for your promise; I say, 'When will you comfort me?' " (Ps 119:81–82). Paul writes, "Now, brothers and sisters, I want to remind you of the gospel" (1 Cor 15:1). While we are making these announcements, there is another hearer, often overlooked, whom we must address; this is where we turn our attention to in the final chapter.

CHAPTER 7

Announcing Jesus to Ourselves

I am glad to boast about my weaknesses, so that the power of Christ can work through me.
—2 Corinthians 12:9 NLT

WE ALL TALK TO OURSELVES. We do. Well, at least *I* do. I talk to myself in a constant internal dialogue called something like "my thoughts." At other times, I say things to myself under my breath—or louder. This happens most often when I'm playing sports and make a mistake or get upset with someone's driving when I'm driving alone. In those moments, words just come out of my mouth. There is something about the energy, the emotion, or the adrenaline that removes an unknown filter that allows a certain place in my guttural internal dialogue to burst forth out of my mouth. To be

honest, the moments that provoke my thought life to spontaneously emerge into my verbal life tend to be words of frustration. But there is another category of words that escape me spontaneously, and those are God's words. I'm not claiming to be a prophet. I'm talking about words that come out subconsciously or perhaps from an even deeper place.

Sometimes words emerge from us instinctively, especially in difficult situations. My neighbor is dying of cancer and has in-home hospice care. He might have a week to live. We don't know. I went out my front door to go on a jog today and as soon as I looked across the street, I was surprised to see a dozen or so cars parked in front of his house. Without any preparation or thought, words emerged from my lips. I said, "Lord, have mercy." Before I could think about why all the cars had showed up suddenly, words came out of my mouth. My instincts spoke for me.

This chapter is an intimate one. Many readers of this book are used to having an audience or a microphone in front of them, listening to the words that come out of their mouths. The previous chapters of this book mostly speak to those situations. This chapter speaks to what we say to ourselves.

You might be the only person that knows these words. The words we say to ourselves can be a hint to what we believe. We need to be careful because emotions can mislead our thoughts, words, and deeds. We also shouldn't fear them, especially because it is impossible to turn them off.

Nearly two decades ago, some friends asked me to speak to about five hundred youth at an evangelistic weekend camp. This was the first time I was asked to do this. I was honored and equally scared out of my mind. I felt a lot of pressure to live up to the expectations of the organizers and the inevitable comparisons I would make with my own life-changing experience at a similar camp. I put an enormous amount of time and effort into my preparations. I interviewed speakers I admired, I pored over the Scriptures, and I went regularly to a local prayer retreat center. I did everything I could to be ready. As ready as I was, one piece of advice from a mentor kept repeating in my thoughts. He told me that one of the most important parts of delivering excellent evangelistic messages was to be passionate for Christ. He told me I really needed to *feel* what I was trying to say to my audience. It was good advice, but I might have overdone it.

The key moment of the weekend was on Saturday night when I would speak in-depth on Christ's death on the cross. I made careful plans to saturate myself with the passion that I felt I needed for that night. When I arrived at the camp, a friend helped me unload my luggage from my car. "What is that for?" he asked. I replied, "Oh, nothing really." He responded, "Really? Why would you need a mini-TV and DVD player for our camp?" As we carried my things to my room, I changed the subject, and it didn't come up again.

Fortunately, the first few talks at the camp went well. Saturday afternoon came, and I initiated my plan. I lugged my mini-TV and DVD player down to the dimly lit basement of the retreat center and settled in. I inserted the DVD into the player and pushed play on the recently released movie *The Passion of the Christ*. For the next two hours and seven minutes, I watched transfixed, and I attempted to soak up all the emotion and passion that I could. And I did. Several times through those two hours, I came to tears as I watched the movie and reflected on Christ's sacrifice. I was a mess. But, oh boy, was I ready to deliver my well-prepared talk with passion. The only problem was the timing of

the camp schedule. I walked out of the basement ready to explode with evangelistic passion, but it was a sunny day during free time at the camp. We had an hour until dinner, then another hour at a leaders' meeting, and then finally our worship service. By the time I spoke, the movie-induced passion had worn off. Nonetheless, I delivered my message as best as I could.

It didn't take me much time after the camp was finished to see my mistake. I had attempted to inject passion and authenticity into my soul as if it were some sort of evangelistic performance-enhancing drug. I look back at that moment with fondness for my naivety. I'm not against the passionate proclamation of the gospel; I think it can help, but it isn't necessary. The only thing that is necessary to proclaim the gospel is the word of God.

COMFORTABLY NUMB

Later, I began to wonder: why did I feel the need to inject artificial passion into my proclamation of the gospel? I now recognize that one reason I felt the need to be more emotive in my presentation of the gospel was because, if I'm being honest, even then, I didn't feel as vibrant and excited about

the gospel as I did when I first came to faith. I felt like the Lord's words to the church in Ephesus applied to me: "But I have this complaint against you. You don't love me or each other as you did at first!" (Rev 2:4). I don't mean this in an either/or way, as if, at first, I loved the Lord and the gospel and then all of a sudden I didn't. Instead, it was a matter of degrees. I could tell that I had slipped a little bit in my external exuberance for my faith. I had the same passion internally, but it worked its way out externally in a more subdued way. The Spirit continued to work in me but in different ways than at first, and when I needed to stand in front of people, I felt exposed—like I needed something extra, something I didn't have.

A few years ago, I picked Paul and David up from Sky Harbor Airport in my hometown of Phoenix, Arizona. I had been their youth group leader when Erin and I lived in Spokane, Washington. When Erin and I moved back to Phoenix, they came to visit us. It was Paul's and David's first time to the southwest, and after we got off the freeway near our home, their mouths dropped and they simultaneously said, "Wow!" I didn't know what they were so excited about. Then

David said, "Paul, look! There's another one!" I was still confused. Paul said, "Oh, I see it!" I looked around and nothing looked out of the ordinary to me. I asked them what they were excited about. Paul finally said, "The cactuses!" They grabbed their cameras and started taking pictures while we drove by cactus after cactus. They were in awe because it was the first time they had seen a cactus in their life. Not me. I grew up thinking cactuses were kind of like weeds; they just grow everywhere and are a bit of a nuisance since you have to avoid them, especially the jumping cholla that fall on the ground, stick to your shoe, and jab you in the ankle if you aren't careful. My life-long familiarity with cactuses numbed me to their enticing strangeness and raw beauty. Paul and David helped me to notice them again.

Those of us who preach the gospel repeatedly have a hard time hearing it ourselves when we say it. Repetition can build up gospel calluses in our hearts. We become so familiar with the words, the ideas, and the responses the gospel receives that it doesn't always catch our attention like it did at first. I'm not saying this is right, universal, or even bad in any definitive way. I'm saying that if you have

experienced this, you aren't alone. As we care for souls by delivering the feast of the gospel, our own soul often goes hungry.

EVANGELISTIC CALLUSES AND LOOFAHS

Evangelistic calluses can also build up in the presence of sin. Thorough pastoral ministry brings us into proximity with the sins of others. Because of this, we learn to guard ourselves in order to keep emotional and spiritual distance from people as a natural, and mostly healthy, tactic to sustain ourselves over the long haul. I'm embarrassed to confess that after a few decades of ministry, it takes hearing a pretty vulgar and disruptive sin to shake me up. Some of the things I hear about today that made me blush and cry in my first years of ministry now feel a bit like business as usual. I don't think this is a good thing, but I know I'm not alone in this experience. When we minister to people and encounter their sin, we reannounce the gospel to them, not to save them again, but to remind them of the confidence they have in Christ's finished work. But in doing so, we can add additional calluses to our hearts if we aren't careful.

My own sin forms some of the deepest calluses, which numb me to hearing the gospel. I

couldn't possibly count the number of times that I've headed to an evangelistic activity while carrying an enormously guilty conscience due to my own sin, whether it was recent sin or from the distant past. A common refrain I hear in my head in those moments is, "Sean, how in the world could you possibly share 'good news' when you are the epitome of 'bad news'? You are such a hypocrite." I know, in theory, how to respond to that devilish voice, but fatigue sometimes gets the best of me, and it robs me of sharing the gospel wholeheartedly.

It took me many years to realize what the dried-spaghetti thing hanging in my shower was for. I learned that it was called a "loofah," and it is designed to scrub away dead and dying skin. It was designed to remove calluses. And, as it turns out, it does a great job. It took me many years to realize that my delivery of the good news is smoother and I enjoy it more if I scrub my life through the ongoing discipline of confession. I wish I could say that I had a naturally strong urge to confess my sins to the Lord, but I don't. My natural urge to confess is present but low. In an ironic twist, the devilish lies I hear when I announce the word of God, especially in evangelism, motivates me to confess my sins. Confession turns the table of lies on its

head and frees me to evangelize with increased zeal. Confession scrubs away calluses from my heart and allows me to feel the life-giving word of God. Confession helps me say, "Devil! I know my sins very well, but you'll have to talk with Jesus— he has all my sin!"[70]

I highly recommend confessing sin to the Lord regularly, perhaps at least once per day. I also recommend confessing your sins with others, as appropriate. Traditions vary, but I have personally found much callus-removing freedom in structured corporate confession. This can be as simple as praying the Lord's Prayer slowly and intentionally—try using pauses between each petition. Or consider the prayer of confession below from the Book of Common Prayer:

> Most merciful God, we confess that we have sinned against you in thought, word, and deed, by what we have done, and by what we have left undone. We have not loved you with our whole heart; we have not loved our neighbors as ourselves. We are truly sorry and we humbly repent. For the sake of your Son Jesus Christ, have mercy on us and forgive us; that we may

delight in your will, and walk in your
ways, to the glory of your Name. Amen.[71]

When I announce the gospel to myself in the light
of my own sin, it helps me to hear it better when
I announce it to others.

Comparing to No One

When I was in graduate school in Scotland, my
family and I came to love the television advertising or "adverts" as they say. The adverts were fun
because they seemed a bit exotic to us. Many of
the products advertised were similar to the ones
we knew in the United States, but there were different brands and the products sometimes had
different features that made them unique. There is
one aspect of UK adverts that my family continues
to talk about today. Have you ever seen a commercial that makes a claim such as "93 percent of dog
owners say their dog's breath is fresher with XYZ
dog biscuits?" In the UK, adverts that make those
sorts of claims reveal their sample size. So, in the
corner of every commercial with a claim like that,
you see the raw data. For example, it might say,
"93 out of 100 dog owners responded affirmatively
to this question in June 2020." My family had a

lot of fun spotting large claims that were based on small surveys; we made it into a bit of a game. We learned to recognize the importance of transparency in advertising, a feature that is less common in America.

I play a dangerous game whenever I compare my evangelistic pursuits to others' works. Nothing good for my heart can come from this comparison. In fact, when I do this, I further numb myself to the good news. This can happen on a small scale. For example, for about a decade I served in an evangelistic ministry alongside my good friend Danny. Danny is one of the best humans I've ever known in my life, and he is a great evangelist. But there were many times when I would hear a student share their testimony and I selfishly expected the testimony to highlight many of the efforts and sacrifices I made to serve the student, only to have my name mentioned zero times and Danny's name said many times. I know how shallow my anecdote is, but I share it because experiences like this make it harder for me to experience the power of the gospel in my own life. It was no fault of Danny's, or the gospel, or the Spirit. It was my fault because I chose to

compare myself to Danny and expected credit for God's work.

I love numbers and spreadsheets; this is perhaps the worst formula possible for the "comparison game." My undergrad degree is in engineering, and my first career was as a product manager. Numbers and spreadsheets are my second language. Because of this, I collect a lot of data on how many students and leaders have come to our events and camps, as well as how many people have been trained and other details. This data can be incredibly useful, but one place it isn't useful is if it is used to build my self-worth. Over the years, I found that I silently—and sometimes audibly—compared my "data" to others' numbers. But whenever I started feeling good about myself because of some recent uptick in our numbers, I would stumble across the annual report of a well-known Christian ministry magazine and learn about the top growing churches and ministries in the country. These reports made my efforts look like failures. This process further numbs my ears to hear the gospel in my own life because I become overly focused and disappointed by the gospel "success rate" in other people's lives.

To hear the gospel in my own life I have found that, as strange as it might sound, I benefit from detaching myself from the outcome of the gospel in other people's lives. Common sense tells us to forget our losses, but I'm also urging you, if you want to hear the gospel clearer, forget your wins. Paul explained to the Philippian church how he learned to view past "righteousness" differently: "But whatever were gains to me I now consider loss for the sake of Christ. What is more, I consider everything a loss because of the surpassing worth of knowing Christ Jesus my Lord, for whose sake I have lost all things. I consider them garbage, that I may gain Christ" (Phil 3:7–8). We experience the goal of the gospel, which is knowing Jesus Christ, when we give up comparing or finding any merit in our own works.

Jesus sent Judas out with power and authority to proclaim the kingdom of God alongside the other disciples (Luke 9:1–2). Later, Satan entered Judas (Luke 22:3). A Satan-filled person can also be a person who Jesus empowered to proclaim the kingdom of God with authority. Even the demons believe that there is one God (Jas 2:19). Judas and the demons had the facts straight. What Judas

failed to do, along with the demons, was to *hear* the message they were able to announce to others. Even someone committing a crime can proclaim Jesus is the Son of God, but unless they know Jesus as their Lord, they do not understand the message they proclaim. One young man I mentored never recovered from the advice his father gave him while he repeatedly cheated on his mother. "Son," he said, "do as I say, not as I do." I knew from many years of knowing the young man that the dad often said the right things to his son. Yet, the dad ruined countless lives along the way, including his own.

The reason we need to announce the gospel to ourselves isn't because of how it will affect our ministries. That is a terrible reason to remain faithful to the Lord. The gospel will bear fruit all on its own. The reason we need to announce the gospel is because we need the gospel, we need Jesus—that's it. I'm not trying to downplay the catastrophic pain and damage inflicted when gospel ministers fail those who trust them, but even in those avoidable disasters, the Lord is still the Lord of all, and his plans cannot be thwarted (Job 42:2). Nothing can diminish the word of God.

How to Discover
Times of Refreshing

Peter told the Israelites at Solomon's Colonnade that they had caused Jesus's suffering through their own ignorance. Peter gave them simple instructions: "Repent, then, and turn to God, so that your sins may be wiped out, that times of refreshing may come from the Lord" (Acts 3:19). Peter knew from firsthand experience what it was like to proclaim the good news of the kingdom (Luke 9:1–2) while failing to hear and really believe it himself. Peter denied the Lord three times. If anyone knew what it felt like to be refreshed by the Lord, it was Peter; the Lord Jesus Christ reinstated Peter and re-invited him to "follow me," just as he did when they first met (Matt 4:18; John 21:19).

So, take it from Peter the expert: be refreshed, repent, and turn to God. All of us have failed to fully embrace the gospel, lest we think that Paul's explanation that "all have sinned and fall short of the glory of God" doesn't apply to Christians (Rom 3:23). We needed the gospel when we came to faith, we need the gospel today, and we need the gospel tomorrow. Yes, I confessed that "Jesus is Lord" in the past, but I say it again today, and I plan to say it tomorrow and for eternity. Repentance is not

simply a task to undertake on a case-by-case basis in response to individual sins; it is an ongoing and perpetual task to continually recalibrate our wandering minds and hearts to the truth that Jesus is Lord. I believe the God who made heaven and earth was born of a virgin (for me) and died on the cross (for me) and rose again from the dead (for me!). I will not be deceived. The truth is in me: I am a sinner; I continue to confess my sin. And an equal truth is in me: I am purified from all unrighteousness (1 John 1:8–9).

One way to announce the gospel to ourselves is to follow a structured Scripture and prayer plan. For many of us in ministry, there are few people checking in on us to walk with us and nudge us in our Scripture reading and prayer. I strongly recommend committing to a daily predetermined Scripture and prayer routine. If we do this, we will encounter the gospel regularly and be provided a chance to believe it again and again.

Another way to hear the gospel is to respond to our sins when we notice them. When you sin, confess it, and receive the Lord's forgiveness. When you do this, you announce and respond to the gospel. Christ paid the price of our sin in full, his mercies never run out, as Hebrews teaches us: "Let

us then approach God's throne of grace with confidence, so that we may receive mercy and find grace to help us in our time of need" (Heb 4:16).

A final recommendation is to force yourself to take time for the Lord to speak to you and show you your ongoing need for the gospel. The Lord provided an event specially designed for this purpose: the Lord's Supper. During the Lord's Supper, "everyone ought to examine themselves before they eat of the bread and drink from the cup" (1 Cor 11:28). Many churches I visit violate this commandment. I fear that this command is overlooked because the ministers have not made self-examination a part of their own lives, and this weakness, like osmosis, seeps into how they conduct the Lord's Supper.

Ask yourself this: are you the ninety-nine or the one? Are you the one sinner who needs to repent or a member of the ninety-nine righteous persons who do not need to repent? There is only one correct answer. This answer leads to eternal life. Announce it to yourself. Hear the gospel and believe it today so that times of refreshing may come into your life. One of the many privileges and challenges of being a minister is our proximity to the gospel. When we hear the gospel again

and again it can either numb our ears and hearts
if we listen to the lies of Satan, or it can quicken
our heart and soul if we listen to the voice of its
author. At times, I feel that God chose me to be
an evangelist because of my desperate need to be
in great proximity to the repeated announcing of
the gospel. I feel like a person with breathing prob-
lems that lives near the ever-fresh, life-giving, rich
oxygen of the seashore. Perhaps others might not
need the assistance I require, but for me it is good
to surround myself with the gospel. I am thankful
to do the work of an evangelist. I invite you to do
the same.

And you, my child, will be called a prophet
    of the Most High;
    for you will go on before the Lord to
        prepare the way for him,
to give his people the knowledge of salvation
    through the forgiveness of their sins,
because of the tender mercy of our God,
    by which the rising sun will come to us
        from heaven
to shine on those living in darkness
    and in the shadow of death,
to guide our feet into the path of peace.

Luke 1:76–79

CHAPTER 8

Three Laws for Evangelism for the Care of Souls

In the preceding chapters, I did my best to present a guide for evangelism that cares for souls. Some readers will be satisfied and have plenty to chew on but others will want a bit more. I've provided a scriptural and pastoral approach to evangelism. Yet, some will still ask, "What do I do now?" The literature on evangelism is saturated with how-to guides, but we must not forget the people behind our task and the God in charge of our task.

I have an uncomfortable relationship with evangelistic how-to literature, even though God has certainly used the plans of salvation and

spiritual laws to deliver the good news. While I take issue with some of the substance of these materials, my main concern is for what they assume. In isolation, these materials attempt to provide salvation through *information*. Salvation comes not through information, but through an encounter with our Savior Jesus Christ delivered by members of his church via his word through the power of the Holy Spirit and the plan of the Father. Evangelistic strategies risk confusing words from an argument with words from a person—the *Persons* of our triune God usually delivered by the person(s) proclaiming the word of God. To respond to evangelism isn't to respond to an argument but a person. And that means evangelism is more than just information.

With this in mind, here's a new set of "laws," or spiritual guidelines one can follow when evangelizing. (These laws do not replace the groundwork laid throughout this book.)

Law 1: Listen

Evangelism thrives when Christians listen attentively to God's word, to those God puts in our lives, and to our own lives.

Law 2: Announce

Evangelism thrives when (after listening) we announce that Jesus is Lord in a way that adapts to what we heard (this requires wisdom).

Law 3: Repeat

Evangelism thrives when we develop a regular habit of listening and announcing that Jesus is Lord.

EXPLANATION OF THE THREE LAWS FOR EVANGELISM FOR THE CARE OF SOULS

Law 1: Listen

Evangelism thrives when Christians listen attentively to God's Word, to those God puts in our lives, and to our own lives.

Evangelists do what no pamphlet can do. Evangelists listen. Throughout this book, I've shown that evangelists who care for souls most often care for souls by listening. The first voice pastors must listen to is the voice of Scripture. Do you want to evangelize your community? Don't head out the door. Turn around. Head straight to your prayer room and allow the word of God to overwhelm you anew. Listen to the word.

After listening to the word, listen to a person. The person you need to listen to is yourself. Have you heard the gospel today? Have you listened to the word to show you that the sin you committed moments ago was taken to the cross and defeated in Christ's resurrection? Have you listened to your excuses for your sin? Have you listened to the shame you load upon yourself? Have you stopped to recognize the lies of Satan in your mind and responded by confronting them with the truths of Christ which set you free? Listen to your life.

Finally, you are prepared to listen to the person whom God places in front of you. Evangelists with Scripture-saturated and renewed souls, hearts, and minds will be best prepared for evangelism. Evangelism, like all ministry, is not a one-size fits all task. A doctor who fails to listen and, instead, prescribes the same medicine for every symptom harms their patients and needs to go back to medical school for retraining. Listen with one ear attuned to the words of the person in front of you and another ear attuned to God's word, being prepared to announce them.

Law 2: Announce

Evangelism thrives when (after listening) we announce that Jesus is Lord in a way that adapts to what we heard (this requires wisdom).

The announcement of the good news is not a predetermined road, a set of laws, or a bridge to cross. The wise announcer is a well-weathered guide with a plethora of routes to the same destination. Most modern map systems provide reliable alternate routes and various means of transportation (car, public transport, walking, etc.) for getting to a destination. The evangelist announces that the crucified Christ Jesus is Lord in a variety of ways (see chapter 4) with wisdom guided by the Spirit. This announcement happens on Sundays during baptisms, Communion, and absolution, as well as in after-church parking lot conversations. This announcement happens as parents tuck in their children before they drift off to sleep. In backyards, offices, text messages, pizza parlors, or train stations—if we are listening spiritually, an announcement that Jesus is Lord, in all its forms, might be the best next words off your lips.

Law 3: Repeat

Evangelism thrives when we develop a regular habit of listening and announcing that Jesus is Lord.

Evangelists who care for souls listen and announce the gospel repeatedly. Evangelists listen to the word of God, their own lives, and the lives others as often and as repetitively as they can. They announce that Jesus is Lord like a broken record. Evangelism is not a one-time occurrence followed up with discipleship. Evangelism is discipleship, and discipleship is evangelism. Find as many opportunities to listen and announce that Christ is Lord. There is a throne before the Lord in front of which day and night the phrase will never stop: " 'Holy, holy, holy is the Lord God Almighty,' who was, and is, and is to come" (Rev 4:8). Join the never-ending chorus that awaits us when we come before the throne of the Lord.

Resources

> Packer, J. I. *Evangelism and the Sovereignty of God*. IVP, 2012.

The title of this classic book accurately reflects its contents. This book is not a blueprint for evangelistic tactics. Instead, Packer's book discusses the sovereignty of God from a Reformed perspective and how that relates to the responsibility of Christians to evangelize. Packer does his best to untangle a seeming contradiction between God's sovereignty and human responsibility in evangelism. In the end, he concludes that a comprehensible solution is not available to humans. As he explains this, he provides practical wisdom and principles for evangelists. Reformed Christians frequently list this as one of their favorite books on evangelism, but it also has much to say to evangelists in all traditions.

> Green, Michael. *Evangelism in the Early Church.* Eerdmans, 2004.

This academic book provides an in-depth analysis of evangelism in the early church. Green provides numerous primary source details and offers thoughtful analysis on how the early church shared the gospel and initiated new believers into Christianity. This book will be a difficult read for many modern evangelicals because Green shows that the early church grew astronomically through methods very different from modern approaches. Generally speaking, early church evangelism occurred through non-Christians becoming interested in the countercultural lifestyles of early Christians; then, when the non-Christian asked about the Christian's faith, a slow process of initiation began that culminated in baptism prior to becoming a member of the church.

> Bright, Bill. "Have You Heard of the Four Spiritual Laws?"

This is not a book, but its influence on modern evangelism, especially among evangelicals, is hard to overstate. Its publishers claim that over one hundred million copies have been sold and it has

been translated into "all of the major languages in the world." I know many mature Christians who credit the "Four Spiritual Laws" with helping them understand the gospel and come to faith in Jesus Christ. Yet, the way it presents the gospel has received criticism for proclaiming a reductionist gospel focused on individualism. While I don't outright recommend this booklet for evangelism due to its reductionism, familiarity with it is extremely useful.

> McKnight, Scot. *The King Jesus Gospel: The Original Good News Revisited.* Zondervan, 2016.

This book takes dead aim at evangelistic approaches that present the gospel as simply "how to get to heaven" or "how to get saved." McKnight rightly shows how the modern conception of much of evangelism is off course and reductionistic. He reaches further than prudent in his attempt to explain the Nicene Creed as an exegesis of 1 Corinthians 15, but his general point is taken and helpful. This book is a readable antidote for evangelists who are concerned about the modern reduction of the gospel.

> Abraham, William J. *The Logic of Evangelism.*
> Eerdmans, 1989.

Abraham has his finger on the heartbeat of many of the strengths and weaknesses of modern evangelism. Some readers might struggle with this book since his approach is more academic than most books on this list. While he is critical of some of the practices and principles of evangelism, he responds with careful and abundant constructive insight. He joins a chorus of modern authors who believe that modern evangelism needs to reorient their proclamation of the gospel toward the kingdom of God that is already present but not yet fully here.

> Coleman, Robert E. *The Master Plan of Evangelism.* Revell, 2010.

This is a classic book on evangelism, but not in the way you might expect from its title. This book explores strategies and tactics for leadership and discipleship in order to accomplish a sustainable and growing evangelistic ministry. Coleman spends little time explaining the gospel or ways to present the gospel to people. I should add that the book is a bit dated and embedded with a strong "wartime" mentality that pervaded American

Christianity when Coleman wrote the book. This book is most helpful for churches and training organizations seeking to develop leadership amid evangelistic activities.

> Lewis, C. S. *Mere Christianity.* Harper Collins, 2002.

When *Christianity Today* declared *Mere Christianity* the "book of the century," they provided a simple explanation: this book is "the best case for the essentials of orthodox Christianity in print."[72] This book presents a strong case for Christianity as it discusses human nature, common conceptions of God, Christian behavior, and an introduction to the Trinity. Aside from the content Lewis's book delivers, evangelists can mine this book as an exemplar of presenting Christianity in an engaging way people will hear. It is both an example of excellent evangelism and an excellent training tool in evangelism.

> Pope-Levison, Priscilla. *Models of Evangelism.* Baker Academic, 2020.

This very practical book discusses eight approaches to evangelism, such as personal evangelism, small group evangelism, and visitation evangelism. Each

chapter covers a different model and includes its biblical basis, theological themes, historical development, step-by-step ways to implement, and an appraisal of the model. While some of the models will be more useful to readers than others (for instance, her chapter on evangelism through media may not be as useful to some people), her systematic analysis of each approach highlights features of evangelism ministers might overlook otherwise.

> Athanasius. *On the Incarnation*. St. Vladimirs Seminary Press, 2012.

On the Incarnation is one of the most important works of Christology of all time written by one of the church's most significant theologians. At first, it might not appear to be relevant for modern evangelism since Athanasius wrote it in the fourth century, but it is very useful today. Athanasius's purpose for writing this book was to explain the purpose of the cross—which is a topic at the heart of evangelism. Athanasius begins his book with a discussion of creation and then moves on to sin, the cross, the resurrection, and an explanation of how people are changed by this message. Modern evangelists would be wise to fortify their understanding of the

gospel through a deeper understanding of Christ's work and divinity with this classic text written seventeen hundred years ago.

> ⯈ Keller, Timothy. *The Reason for God: Belief in an Age of Skepticism*. Penguin Books, 2008.

Keller's book is one of the best modern popular-level apologetics books available. Keller forged his approach out of many years of pastoral ministry in a secular context. Keller explores seven of the most common objections and doubts about Christianity before presenting seven reasons to believe. It is not a book about evangelism but a book that does evangelism. In this way, it is similar to Lewis's *Mere Christianity*.

> ⯈ Smith, Gordon T. *Transforming Conversion: Rethinking the Language and Contours of Christian Initiation*. Baker Academic, 2010.

Smith's book is one of the best comprehensive treatments of the topic of conversion, written in a careful but accessible way. He shows how conversion has been understood in the history of the church, and this information lays the groundwork

for us to understand that much of modern evangelism is derivative of revivalism. Smith builds on his historical work to show how we can deepen modern Christian initiation by learning from the past.

Notes

1. For an overview, see Thomas S. Kidd, *Who Is an Evangelical?: The History of a Movement in Crisis* (Yale University Press, 2019).

2. Barth said, "It was the gospel at gun-point. ... He preached the law, not a message to make one happy. He wanted to terrify people. ... It was illegitimate to make the gospel law or to 'push' it like an article for sale. ... We must leave the good God freedom to do his own work." Eberhard Busch, *Karl Barth: His Life from Letters and Autobiographical Texts*, trans. John Bowden (Fortress Press, 1976), 446.

3. Charles G. Finney, *Lectures on Revival*, ed. L. G. Parkhurst (Bethany House Publishers, 1988), 167–72.

4. Finney, *Lectures on Revival*, 171.

5. Elisha Coles, *An English Dictionary* (Peter Parker, 1717). Surrounding the definition of evangelism, following the older English of the dictionary (evangelism) are the words "Evangeliques: a sort of reformers not much differing form Lutherans," "evangelistary: a pulpit; also the office of an,"

"evangelist: one that doth," "evangelize: write or bring," "evangelium: the gospel, good news."

6. The third edition of Wesley's English dictionary published in 1777 includes the words "evangelical: belonging or agreeable to the gospel," and "evangelist: a preacher or writer of the gospel," but it does not include an entry for "evangelism." John Wesley, *The Complete English Dictionary* (R. Hawes, 1777).

7. The Student Volunteer Movement began in the 1880s and was led by John R. Mott (missions advocate, world president of the YMCA, and Nobel Peace Prize winner). Its motto, "The Evangelization of the World in This Generation," catalyzed the discussion of evangelism in a new way at the beginning of the nineteenth century. John R. Mott, *The Evangelization of the World in This Generation* (London: Student Volunteer Missionary Union, 1900); Dana L. Robert, "The Origin of the Student Volunteer Watchword: 'The Evangelization of the World in This Generation,' " *International Bulletin of Missionary Research* 10, no. 4 (1986): 146–49; See also, William J. Abraham, *The Logic of Evangelism* (Eerdmans, 1989), 40.

8. For examples of the history of "evangelism," see: Green, *Evangelism in the Early Church*; John Mark Terry, *Evangelism: A Concise History* (Broadman & Holman, 1994); Robert G. Tuttle, *The Story of*

Evangelism: A History of the Witness to the Gospel (Abingdon, 2006).

9. Susan Grove Eastman, *Feasting on the Word: Preaching the Revised Common Lectionary: Year A*, ed. David L. Bartlett and Barbara Brown Taylor (Westminster John Knox, 2011), 169.

10. Raymond F. Collins, "Nathanael (Person)," in *The Anchor Yale Bible Dictionary* (Doubleday, 1992), 1030.

11. Merrill C. Tenney and Richard N. Longenecker, *The Expositor's Bible Commentary: John and Acts*, ed. Frank E. Gaebelein (Zondervan, 1981), 186.

12. James A. Brooks, "Nicodemus," in *Eerdmans Dictionary of the Bible*, ed. David Noel Freedman, Allen C. Myers, and Astrid B. Beck (Eerdmans, 2000), 963.

13. The rich young ruler is the first one to use the phrase "eternal life" in the Gospel of Matthew; outside of this episode, it only occurs once more, in Matthew 25:46. We may wonder why he asked for "eternal life." To answer this question, we need to go back one chapter to Jesus's teaching about causing little ones to stumble (Matt 18:6–9). In this passage, Jesus warns of being "thrown into eternal fire." This passage, like Jesus's words to the rich young ruler, speaks of "entering" life rather than "having" or "holding" life. Additionally, in Matthew 19, Jesus was speaking about little children entering the kingdom of

heaven (19:13–14) when "just then" the rich young ruler came up to Jesus to ask him about eternal life. The parallels between these passages underline the importance of "entering" eternal life rather than "having" or "holding" eternal life as an object.

14. For a good summary of the options, see D. A. Carson, *The Gospel According to John*, The Pillar New Testament Commentary (Eerdmans, 1991), 191–96.

15. Ezekiel 36:25–27 captures how God planned to accomplish this in a unified movement: "I will sprinkle clean water on you, and you will be clean; I will cleanse you from all your impurities and from all your idols. I will give you a new heart and put a new spirit in you; I will remove from you your heart of stone and give you a heart of flesh. And I will put my Spirit in you and move you to follow my decrees and be careful to keep my laws."

16. Frederick Dale Bruner, *The Gospel of John: A Commentary* (Eerdmans, 2012), 180.

17. Calvin, John. *Calvin's Commentaries,* translated by William Pringle (Baker Books, 2009), 16:108.

18. John Calvin, *Commentary on the Book of the Prophet Isaiah*, trans. William Pringle, vol. 7, Calvin's Commentaries (Baker Books, 2009), 216.

19. Frederick Buechner, *Wishful Thinking: A Theological ABC* (HarperCollins, 1973), 73.

20. Calvin, *Commentary on the Book of the Prophet Isaiah*, 7:214.

21. Calvin, *Commentary on the Book of the Prophet Isaiah*, 7:217.

22. Robert W. Yarbrough, *The Letters to Timothy and Titus*, ed. D. A. Carson, Pillar New Testament Commentary (Eerdmans, 2018), 441–42.

23. Some Anglicans follow the tradition of the Eastern Orthodox veneration of the Gospels as an icon of Christ.

24. Howard E. Galley, *Ceremonies of the Eucharist: A Guide to Celebration* (Cowley Publications, 1989), 85.

25. Margaret Dunlap Gibson, trans., *The Didascalia Apostolorum in English* (Cambridge University Press, 2011), 19.

26. "Constitutions of the Holy Apostles," in *The Ante-Nicene Fathers: Translations of the Writings of the Fathers Down to A.D. 325*, vol. 7 (reprint, Hendrickson, 1994), 421.

27. Eusebius, "Church History," in *Nicene and Post-Nicene Fathers: Second Series*, vol. 1 (Hendrickson, 1994), 141.

28. Eusebius, "Church History," 169.

29. Origen, "Commentary on the Gospel of John," in *Nicene and Post-Nicene Fathers: Second Series*, vol. 9 (Hendrickson, 1994), 298–99.

30. For example, see Ignatius (*To the Trallians*, 9), Irenaeus (*Against Heresies*, 1.10.1, 2.4.1–2), the

Apostolic Tradition of Hippolytus, Tertullian (*Prescription Against Heretics*, 13) and others.

31. Tertullian, "The Prescription against Heretics," in in *Nicene and Post-Nicene Fathers: Second Series*, vol. 3 (Hendrickson, 1994), 250.

32. Martin Luther, "Preface to the New Testament" (1546), *Luther Works* 35:360.

33. Gerhard O. Forde, *Where God Meets Man: Luther's Down-To-Earth Approach to the Gospel* (Augsburg, 1972), 32.

34. William J. Abraham, "A Theology of Evangelism: The Heart of the Matter," in *The Study of Evangelism: Exploring a Missional Practice of the Church*, ed. Paul Wesley Chilcote and Laceye C. Warner (Eerdmans, 2008), 29.

35. George Whitefield, *A Further Account of God's Dealings with the Reverend Mr. George Whitefield* (W. Strahan, 1747), 19.

36. Over 92 percent were Anglican, roughly 1 percent Roman Catholic, and the rest were nonconformists. Clive D. Field, "Counting Religion in England and Wales: The Long Eighteenth Century, c. 1680–c. 1840," *The Journal of Ecclesiastical History* 63, no. 4 (2012): 711.

37. For an example of this in Whitefield's ministry, see: Sean McGever, *Born Again: The Evangelical Theology of Conversion in John Wesley and George Whitefield* (Lexham Press, 2020), 110–13.

38. Finney, *Lectures on Revival*, 13.

39. Finney, *Lectures on Revival*, 14.

40. Finney, *Lectures on Revival*, 167.

41. Finney, *Lectures on Revival*, 171.

42. Finney, *Lectures on Revival*, 236.

43. Charles L. Thompson, *Times of Refreshing: A History of American Revivals from 1740 to 1877, with Their Philosophy and Methods* (Golden Censer Company, 1878), 384.

44. Paul Harrison Chitwood, "The Sinner's Prayer: An Historical and Theological Analysis" (unpublished PhD diss., The Southern Baptist Theological Seminary, 2001), 42–61.

45. Bryan P. Stone, *Finding Faith Today* (Cascade Books, 2018), vii–viii.

46. Stone, *Finding Faith Today*, 5.

47. Stone, *Finding Faith Today*, 15.

48. Stone, *Finding Faith Today*, 213.

49. John Finney, *Finding Faith Today: How Does It Happen?* (British and Foreign Bible Society, 1992).

50. Stone, *Finding Faith Today*, 81.

51. Stone, *Finding Faith Today*, 214.

52. Ryan P. Burge, *The Nones: Where They Came From, Who They Are, and Where They Are Going* (Fortress, 2021), 69–70.

53. Burge, *The Nones*, 48.

54. Burge, *The Nones*, 128.

55. Stone, *Finding Faith Today*, 213.

56. Abraham, *The Logic of Evangelism*, 57.

57. Mark Ireland and Mike Booker, *Making New Disciples: Exploring the Paradoxes of Evangelism* (Society for Promoting Christian Knowledge, 2015), 78.

58. There is renewed interest in the practice of catechesis with Christian initiation. A liturgical-ecumenical consensus regarding the sequence of baptism, confirmation, and Eucharist with continual catechesis and continual formation has gained increasing attention outside of liturgical traditions. For further details regarding liturgical Christian initiation in the church today, including Roman Catholic, Episcopal, and Lutheran churches, see Maxwell E. Johnson, *The Rites of Christian Initiation: Their Evolution and Interpretation* (Liturgical Press, 2007), 375–450.

59. Stone, *Finding Faith Today*, 21.

60. Martin Luther, "The Magnificat" (1521), *Luther Works* 21:299. See also Luther's *Small Catechism* on article 3 of the Apostles' Creed.

61. Martin Luther, "Another Short Sermon on the Feast of Mary's Visitation to Elizabeth" (1527), in *D. Martin Luthers Werke, Kritische Gesamtausgabe*, 73 vols. (Weimar: Hermann Böhlaus Nachfolger, 1883–2009), 17,2:460.3–6, 15–18.

62. T. L. Osborn, *Soulwinning: Out Where the Sinners Are* (Osborn Evangelistic Association, 1967), 88, 94.

63. Finney, *Finding Faith Today: How Does It Happen?*, 25.

64. Stone, *Finding Faith Today*, 15.

65. Stone, *Finding Faith Today*, 15.

66. Charles Spurgeon, *Spurgeon Commentary: Hebrews*, ed. Elliot Ritzema (Lexham Press, 2014), 143.

67. Luther, Martin, *A Short Explanation of Dr. Martin Luther's Small Catechism: A Handbook of Christian Doctrine* (Concordia, 1971), 180

68. "Renewal of Baptismal Vows" in *The Book of Common Prayer* (Anglican Liturgy Press, 2019), 194–95.

69. The Absolution of Sin in "The Holy Eucharist" in *The Book of Common Prayer* (2019), 113, 130.

70. See Martin Luther, "Sermon on the Thirteenth Sunday after Trinity" (1530), in *D. Martin Luthers Werke, Kritische Gesamtausgabe*, 73 vols. (Weimar: Hermann Böhlaus Nachfolger, 1883–2009), 32:102.25–103.4; and Todd R. Hains, *Martin Luther and the Rule of Faith: Reading God's Word for God's People* (IVP Academic, 2022), 97.

71. *The Book of Common Prayer* (Seabury Press, 1979), 116–17.

72. *Books of the Century, Christianity Today*, April 24, 2000, https://www.christianitytoday.com/ct /2000/april24/5.92.html

Works Cited

Abraham, William J. "A Theology of Evangelism: The Heart of the Matter." Page 29 in *The Study of Evangelism: Exploring a Missional Practice of the Church*. Edited by Paul Wesley Chilcote and Laceye C. Warner. Eerdmans, 2008.

——. *The Logic of Evangelism*. Eerdmans, 1989.

"Books of the Century." *Christianity Today*. April 2000. https://www.christianitytoday.com/ct/2000/april24/5.92.html

Brooks, James A. "Nicodemus." Page 963 in *Eerdmans Dictionary of the Bible*. Edited by David Noel Freedman, Allen C. Myers, and Astrid B. Beck. Eerdmans, 2000.

Bruner, Frederick Dale. *The Gospel of John: A Commentary*. Eerdmans, 2012.

Buechner, Frederick. *Wishful Thinking: A Theological ABC*. HarperCollins, 1973.

Burge, Ryan P. *The Nones: Where They Came From, Who They Are, and Where They Are Going*. Fortress, 2021.

Busch, Eberhard. *Karl Barth: His Life from Letters and Autobiographical Texts.* Translated by John Bowden. Fortress Press, 1976.

Calvin, John. *Calvin's Commentaries.* Translated by William Pringle. 22 vols. Baker Books, 2009.

Carson, D. A. *The Gospel According to John. The Pillar New Testament Commentary.* Eerdmans, 1991.

Chitwood, Paul Harrison. "The Sinner's Prayer: An Historical and Theological Analysis." PhD diss., The Southern Baptist Theological Seminary, 2001.

Coles, Elisha. *An English Dictionary.* Peter Parker, 1717.

Collins, Raymond F. "Nathanael (Person)." Page 1030 in vol. 4 of *The Anchor Yale Bible Dictionary.* Edited by David Noel Freedman. 6 vols. New York: Doubleday, 1992.

"Constitutions of the Holy Apostles." Pages 387–509 in vol. 7 of *The Ante-Nicene Fathers: Translations of the Writings of the Fathers Down to A.D. 325.* Reprint, Hendrickson, 1994.

The Book of Common Prayer. Seabury Press, 1979.

The Book of Common Prayer. Anglican Liturgy Press, 2019.

Dunlap Gibson, Margaret, trans. *The Didascalia Apostolorum in English.* Cambridge: Cambridge University Press, 2011.

Eusebius. "Church History." In vol. 1 of *Nicene and Post-Nicene Fathers: Second Series*. Reprint, Hendrickson, 1994.

Field, Clive D. "Counting Religion in England and Wales: The Long Eighteenth Century, c. 1680– c. 1840." *The Journal of Ecclesiastical History* 63, no. 4 (2012): 711.

Finney, Charles G. *Lectures on Revival*. Edited by L. G. Parkhurst. Bethany House Publishers, 1988.

Finney, John. *Finding Faith Today: How Does It Happen?* British and Foreign Bible Society, 1992.

Forde, Gerhard O. *Where God Meets Man: Luther's Down-To-Earth Approach to the Gospel.* Augsburg, 1972.

Galley, Howard E. *Ceremonies of the Eucharist: A Guide to Celebration.* Cowley Publications, 1989.

Green, Michael. *Evangelism in the Early Church*. Rev. ed. Eerdmans, 2004.

Grove Eastman, Susan. *Feasting on the Word: Preaching the Revised Common Lectionary: Year A*. Edited by David L. Bartlett and Barbara Brown Taylor. Westminster John Knox, 2011.

Ireland, Mark. and Mike Booker. *Making New Disciples: Exploring the Paradoxes of Evangelism.* Society for Promoting Christian Knowledge, 2015.

Johnson, Maxwell E. *The Rites of Christian Initiation: Their Evolution and Interpretation.* Liturgical Press, 2007.

Kidd, Thomas S. *Who Is an Evangelical?: The History of a Movement in Crisis.* Yale University Press, 2019.

Luther, Martin. *A Short Explanation of Dr. Martin Luther's Small Catechism: A Handbook of Christian Doctrine.* Concordia, 1971.

——. *D. Martin Luthers Werke, Kritische Gesamtausgabe.* 73 vols. Weimer: Hermann Böhlaus Nachfolger, 1883–2009.

McGever, Sean. *Born Again: The Evangelical Theology of Conversion in John Wesley and George Whitefield.* Lexham Press, 2020.

Mott, John R. *The Evangelization of the World in This Generation.* Student Volunteer Missionary Union, 1900.

Origen, "Commentary on the Gospel of John." Page 298-99 in vol. 9 of *Nicene and Post-Nicene Fathers: Second Series.* Reprint, Hendrickson, 1994.

Osborn, T. L. *Soulwinning: Out Where the Sinners Are.* Tulsa: Osborn Evangelistic Association, 1967.

Robert, Dana L. "The Origin of the Student Volunteer Watchword: 'The Evangelization of the World

in This Generation.'" *International Bulletin of Missionary Research* 10, no. 4 (1986): 146–49.

Spurgeon, Charles. *Spurgeon Commentary: Hebrews.* Edited by Elliot Ritzema. Lexham Press, 2014.

Stone, Bryan P. *Finding Faith Today.* Cascade Books, 2018.

Tenney, Merrill C. and Richard N. Longenecker. *The Expositor's Bible Commentary: John and Acts.* Edited by Frank E. Gaebelein. Zondervan, 1981.

Terry, John Mark. *Evangelism: A Concise History.* Broadman & Holman, 1994.

Tertullian. "The Prescription against Heretics." In vol. 3 of *Nicene and Post-Nicene Fathers: Second Series.* Reprint, Hendrickson, 1994.

Thompson, Charles L. *Times of Refreshing: A History of American Revivals from 1740 to 1877, with Their Philosophy and Methods.* Golden Censer Company, 1878.

Tuttle, Robert G. *The Story of Evangelism: A History of the Witness to the Gospel.* Abingdon, 2006.

Whitefield, George. *A Further Account of God's Dealings with the Reverend Mr. George Whitefield.* London: W. Strahan, 1747.

Yarbrough, Robert W. *The Letters to Timothy and Titus.* Pillar New Testament Commentary. Eerdmans, 2018.

MINISTRY, FOR THE CARE OF SOULS

To learn more about the Lexham Ministry Guides, visit lexhampress.com/lmg

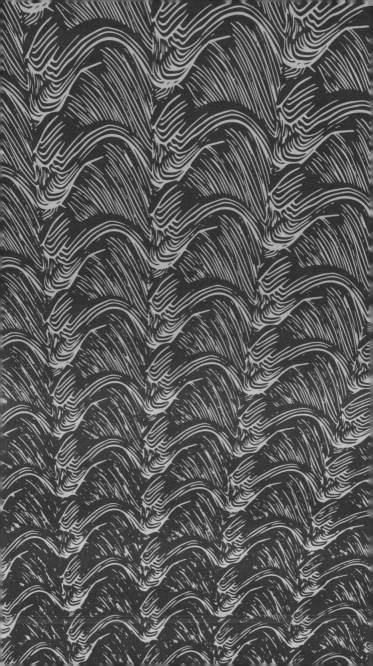

acts of listening and announcing the gospel. He urges us to begin our evangelistic work by listening to ourselves and making sure we apply the gospel and it's beautiful message of freedom to our own lives. These acts of listening and announcing create the basis of being able to truly listen to the person God is placed right in front of us and authentically engage them with the Gospel. I'm looking forward to integrating Sean's ideas into the evangelism strategy of the church I pastor and developing relationships that truly care for the souls of the people God puts in our path."

—J. Owen Carroll,
lead pastor, Ethnos Church, Richardson, Texas

all to better understand the importance and practice of evangelism for the care of souls. A must-read for anyone involved in ministry."

—Marty Gray,
pastor, Ravenhill Presbyterian Church, Belfast,
Northern Ireland

"Sean McGever's *Evangelism: For the Care of Souls* is a thorough, appropriately challenging, and compelling call for all believers to "do the work of an evangelist" (2 Timothy 4:5). Sean's faithfulness to Scripture and the skillful use of insights and perspectives of key voices are wrapped in a warm and inviting narrative style that offers an accessible and unique resource. As much as ever people need to hear and experience the witness and word of Jesus Christ. Evangelism provides not only the encouragement to lovingly engage our neighbor with the good news of Jesus but also equips us for the journey. This is a great book, and I highly recommend it."

—Chap Clark,
affiliate professor of youth, family, and culture,
Fuller Theological Seminary

"Sean's work is unique. This book serves as a powerful reminder that the task of evangelism isn't just about winning converts; it's about relationally caring for the souls of the people we encounter by making our own spiritual health and their spiritual growth a priority. Instead of adding to the multitude of books on evangelism with another method or systematic plan, he advocates for an understanding of the important task of evangelism that centers on relational engagement and the simple

"The role and function of the pastorate involves multiple dimensions of soul-care. One of these facets includes pastors caring for souls through the practice and discipline of evangelism. Sean McGever's *Evangelism: For the Care of Souls* offers pastors a philosophical framework that is both biblical and practical. I found it helpful and you will, too!"

—Matt Queen,
professor and L. R. Scarborough Chair
of Evangelism, Southwestern Baptist
Theological Seminary

"In a sea of step-by-step, programmatic, 'how-to' literature on evangelism, Sean McGever instead offers an incredibly vulnerable look into the ongoing work of God to care for his people through his people. With a shepherd's heart and an impressive knack for storytelling, McGever summons scores of names, places, and anecdotes that are sure to convict—and encourage—even the most inexperienced Christian. The power of this book is the author's ability to identify with the common failings and misconceptions of evangelism in a way that points readers to the Triune God and his word, and not to themselves."

—Obbie Tyler Todd,
pastor, Third Baptist Church, Marion, Illinois

"I have read many books on evangelism that have left me feeling guilty and inadequate for the task. This book, however, left me feeling inspired and assured. Through careful exegesis, insightful reflection, winsome personal stories, and inspiring historical accounts, Sean helps us